Unveiling The Heart
Of Awareness

Books by Bruce Davis, PhD

The Magical Child Within You

Hugs & Kisses

The Heart of Healing

Monastery Without Walls

My Little Flowers

Simple Peace- Spiritual Life of St. Francis of Assisi

The Calling of Joy

The Love Letters of St. Francis and St. Clare of Assisi

Unveiling The Heart Of Awareness

*Contemplative Meditations On
The Journey Of Awakening*

Bruce Davis

UNVEILING THE HEART OF AWARENESS CONTEMPLATIVE MEDITATIONS ON THE JOURNEY OF AWAKENING

iUniverse books may be ordered through booksellers or by contacting:

iUniverse
1663 Liberty Drive
Bloomington, IN 47403
www.iuniverse.com
844-349-9409

Because of the dynamic nature of the Internet, any web addresses or links contained in this book may have changed since publication and may no longer be valid. The views expressed in this work are solely those of the author and do not necessarily reflect the views of the publisher, and the publisher hereby disclaims any responsibility for them.

Any people depicted in stock imagery provided by Getty Images are models, and such images are being used for illustrative purposes only.
Certain stock imagery © Getty Images.

ISBN: 978-1-6632-4762-9 (sc)
ISBN: 978-1-6632-4763-6 (e)

Print information available on the last page.

iUniverse rev. date: 11/16/2022

Contents

Introduction

In challenging times, we are all feeling a need to find more inner resources, to discover our greater awareness to both manage daily life and enjoy more heartfulness, moment to moment. In the time of COVID 2020-2022, many of us were more or less isolated in our homes. Our social activity was greatly limited while our meditative life was offering new opportunities. We could either fall victim to the time and the illness infecting so many or we could use these many months to discover new ways to awaken our hearts, our awareness of life's potential. During this time, I began offering weekly meditations on Zoom to those of our community who have joined us through the years in retreats in America and Europe, especially those who had attended our two retreat centers in Assisi, Italy and at Silent Stay Retreats in California.

Now, more than ever, was the time to deepen our meditation practice and unveil our true nature, the peace and light waiting within us. Do we dare to take the inner journey, the journey into the very heart of our awareness? Some of the meditations in this book would come to me a few days before our Sunday sessions. On my daily walks by the ocean, the meditation rose from the ocean within me. Other meditations came to me just moments before our meeting as I would listen to the silence within. Our Sunday sessions became a verbal endeavor trying to share what was surfacing within. Meanwhile our Sunday circle grew with people joining us in California, other parts of America, Canada, England, Germany, Hungary, Finland, Sweden, Netherlands, India, and many more places. We are a community! Everyone would come and go each week as they pleased. Our world community was present, supporting one another to live best we can in the great silence of our hearts. Together we are exploring the contemplative journey.

The meditations were put into print with little editing. They are simply spontaneous words for the inner experience. They are repetitive, not meant to be read page after page. Each chapter in this book is a meditation, a reflection, a guide, and support. The contemplative journey is a winding river into the great ocean. We unveil all the thoughts, all that is distracting us from the great love, the vastness, the peace within us. As we discover our abundant inner world, we have so much more to offer on our Earthly path. Together we open to the absolute silence, the light of eternity.

Finding the Other Side
in Our Heart

---

*Beneath our busy daily lives, we can find the source of all
peace; the ocean of awareness and silence within the heart.*

It's beautiful that we can sit together in the heart inside our heart.
We are pioneers, exploring the vast realms within. All the religions
on the outside look different. But contemplatives on the inside in
Hinduism, Buddhism, Judaism, Christianity, Sufis, Shamanism,
and Muslims, know we're all making the same journey ... into
the heart inside our heart. When I was in graduate school in
psychology, almost 50 years ago, we were told that we are thoughts
and feelings. Inside these feelings are more feelings and underneath
again other feelings. Our work was to understand, to express, to
experience, and have compassion for these feelings. And that's who
we are. But through the years, we have discovered that we are much
more than our thoughts and feelings. Each of us is a mountain of
awareness. An ocean of awareness. In truth, our thoughts and our
feelings are just the very surface of our awareness. Maybe 5% of
who we are. Most people live in this 5%. And then when they die;
they join the other 95% into this big awareness. It's a shock. They
don't really know or understand. It's such a big experience. People
who've had near death experiences have found that when they go
into their big awareness, it's so big, so much love, so much light and

colors; it's all brilliant. They find themselves coming home. But we don't need to have a heart attack or have an automobile accident and die to go to our big awareness, to come home inside. In fact, the other side is the other side of our mental world. And this is the world of our heart. We are all explorers of the other side. And we don't need the drama of getting sick and dying. We just need the journey, to sit together, and be in the deep heart inside each of us.

We breathe. We feel the entire mountain of awareness of who we are. We breathe and feel the incredible ocean of awareness. So much peace inside, so much vastness. We can come home in this body, in this world in our own heart. This is the journey to come home inside. So, how do we escape this mental world and go to the other side which is really the world of our hearts? We practice letting go, not holding so tightly to our everyday self. Let the pages of our everyday story turn, let the chapters move, let the book continue, we are much more than our story. As we let go, our awareness begins to relax. We go underneath the waves into the ocean of who we are. We spend so much energy trying to control the waves, trying to be comfortable, and we're never very comfortable. Our home is deep inside our hearts. So we practice letting go, offering, letting the thoughts and the feelings just be thoughts and feelings. As we come into the vastness of the silence inside, our thoughts and feelings become smaller and smaller. As we come into the great quiet of our own heart, the challenges in daily life, the obstacles, they get smaller and smaller. As we come deeper and deeper into the stillness of our heart, the daily world has a new perspective, it's not so big. Just little dots in the sky of who we really are. Each of us are pioneers traveling into the other side of our mental world, into the world of our hearts. There's no right or wrong here. Just as the people who have near death experiences find there's no judgment, there's just a great presence of love.

This we can practice now. No judgment. Let our experience just be, and receive this big presence of love. The light is very bright on the other side. The light is so bright in our own hearts... this is Christ. This is our Buddha nature. This is Shiva, all of the wisdom mothers and the goddesses. There is no need to put words to the journey. It's the journey itself that is important. The path gets bigger and bigger. We come deeper and deeper into the beauty of our own heart. We breathe. We offer any thoughts, any distractions, our breath. With the breath, we come deeper and deeper, into the very essence, the very heart of our awareness.

This is our journey, our path. We focus, concentrate on receiving the most-pure heart inside our heart. And here there is another heart. In the distance, the light is small. As we go deeper into the heart, where the heart comes closer to us, the light grows brighter and brighter, so brilliant. This is the other side, which is the world of our heart. So much light... so many rays of colorful light... We breathe and receive the peace through our whole being. It is everywhere. Inside, outside. Our awareness has no beginning, no ending. This is love's body. The body of who we really are. We are held in so much love, peacefulness. We are so much love, quiet. All of our nerves drink the heart essence. Our awareness is washed in light. Quiet... silence. Together we must take this bath again and again. We let the silence wash everything. Wash until the other side is completely present. This side of our own heart.

Here we are with no beginning, no ending. There is no time here. No time, and we are free. No border, no boundary. Just complete freedom of light. Quiet… silence, warm love. We feel the heart inside of our heart unfolding. Expanding everywhere, including the people we live with, the home we live in, the trees and nature. There is no ending. We're remembering the other side, which is this side of our heart. Our awareness keeps unfolding into more and more of itself. We keep coming deeper and deeper and deeper within. It's so beautiful to come home again.

It's special to sit in this beingness, this inner vastness, together. We are more together than together. We support each other. As we receive the pure heart inside our heart, it spreads everywhere through us, into the world. Most people are looking for the divine outside, in their daily story, and they find moments of it. With the waves of so many thoughts and feelings, so much activity going on, it's only moments. The opportunity is to find the divine in our own heart. Our heavy mind becomes lighter and lighter. Our thoughts and feelings are just thoughts and feelings. We get more clear and different perspective. This inner vastness and we see the world differently. We're here to bring our heart, to bring the divine, into the world. We're here to receive as much love as we can. And then we naturally offer it everywhere. Each of us are pioneers into the other side, which is the side of our own heart.

Finding Stability in
the Unknown

*Beneath the crashing waves of thought and busyness
is a vast sea of inner tranquility. Finding this peace
within is the key to stability in an unknown world.*

How do we find stability in these times? How do we find real stability? Everything is changing, everything is moving, our homes, our work, our family, relationships. We're always looking for stability. Here in California, even the ground, the earth, is not stable. We have earthquakes and fires. Something deep inside of us wants stability. So we work on our thoughts, work on our feelings, we try to have strong beliefs, but even so we don't have stability. The waves of daily life are always moving. They're strong, They're loud. There are big winds and smaller winds, currents pulling us in all directions. Life is full of changes. Everything is in movement. Yet yearn for stability. We're called to find stability in the unknown. As we go underneath the waves of daily life, underneath our busy minds and all our feelings, there is the ocean of our being…there is the silence of our hearts. As we let go of looking for stability outside, we turn inward. As we come into the silence of our heart, something here is very stable. There is a vastness, a beingness. As we come deeper inside, we feel more stable. As the waves around us are tossing, turning, and crashing, inside there's this deep calm. As we go deeper into the ocean of our own awareness, as we go further into the silence of our own heart, this calm is more than calm. It is peace. We breathe in this great peace. There's stability here. The waves may be moving and crashing around us. There may be seemingly endless thoughts, but underneath the waves there's this ocean, the depths are pure peace. We breathe into the heart inside our heart. And here there is a great heart. Endless peace.

This peace is stability. It's always present inside, waiting for us. We go into the pure peace that is inside this peace. It is a mountain of stability. This peace is so strong. So true. Our awareness comes home here, and this home is built of total truth. Just being. Peace. No matter what is happening in our lives, this heart inside our heart is here. Present. This big peace inside holds us in the presence of this moment. This moment is our source of stability. Whenever life is spinning out of control, we come back to this moment in our hearts, inside our heart, into the pure, pure, heart, so much vastness… peace.

As we breathe and come deeper and deeper into who we are, we come into the very heart of our awareness. Here there is light. At first it may seem in the distance, small, but it grows bigger and bigger and bigger. This light is so bright. It is everywhere, inside of us, around us, everywhere. This light is our stability. It is so bright, so brilliant, from deep inside the center of our center. This light is our essence. It's who we are. It's God. The very center of the universe is in each of us. We come into the center of the universe inside, with all the planets and the stars, in us and around us. This is stability. So centered, the whole universe is here within us, everywhere. We breathe this light. We are this light.

Our awareness is so free here. This is stability. We just soak into who we really are. We just be in our beingness. There is no limit, no border. We feel our true body, love's body, the body of our great awareness. No beginning, no ending, we deeply relax inside. We kwon.

We are, as we keep spreading more, more, spreading more, more, unfolding, into our own infinite. We concentrate on being the very center of our center, the most-pure heart within our heart. Within this heart is another heart and within even more, more heart. So much divine is everywhere. Our nervous system lets go into the great All. Every nerve lightens up again, just light. We breathe. Our breath in the heart, awareness, the universe... it's all one. This oneness is our stability.

Every day we want to remember to drink from the silence of our own heart. Here is our stability. In the silence of our heart, we discover the full body of our awareness. No beginning, no ending. And in the very heart of our awareness, we are the center of the universe. And out of the heart of our awareness emerges our diamond mind, our pure mind, clarity, stability, light, gentleness, humility, and love. We want to drink from our source every day and remember who we really are. Stability, in these changing times, is a big gift to ourselves, and to each other.

Resurrection and The Cave of Our Heart

The Easter story shows us the steps to spiritual rebirth, regardless of one's religion. All can receive the silence of the chrysalis and emerge renewed.

Resurrection is not something we have to believe in. We don't have to wait until we die to experience resurrection. Resurrection is here now, in us, and with us. The Easter story is beautiful. It gives specific steps toward resurrection. It begins with the last supper, and Christ surrenders to everything that goes on. There are friends and people we thought were friends who are not so friendly. There's love and devotion and betrayal…cruelty. Everything in the human story is included in these few hours. And it's beautiful that God is with us in these hours, no matter how difficult or challenging our life may be. God gives a clear step that he is with us. It's no accident. And Christ surrenders to the whole story, inviting us to surrender to our whole story, just to be with the story. And then he says do not judge them, for they do not know what they do. And this is true for ourselves and everyone in our lives, not to judge them, for they do not know what they do, what we do. And then the next beautiful step.

After the crucifixion, all the crucifixions that each of us go through, big and small, in our lives, He is put into the cave. And we are invited into the cave of our own hearts. We don't know if it's just hours or days. It's not immediate. He's in the cave of the heart, and a great silence. There is nothing here. In these hours, the church, even the altars, are emptied. The churches are no longer church, there's just a big nothing. There's a big silence. In the cave of our heart, we sit, in this great silence. And God is here. Somehow, the rock, the stone, is pushed away. And we emerge from the cave of our heart, from this great silence. There's just so much light. Infinite light. So much light. And first it's the women, the women disciples recognize Christ. And that is true in our lives, too. It's the women, it's the feminine, it's those who are feeling, that recognize us. And then Christ is in the world and yet he is in another world. This story is beautiful, very mysterious, true for all of us. After we are transformed in the silence, in the cave of our heart, we emerge into the light. And we are not the same. We are changed. We are in this world and yet there is another world. So much light and so much presence, and so much peace. And such a deep, deep, beautiful love.

The Easter story gives us clear steps. We are invited to follow these steps into the resurrection of our own awareness. When Christ emerged from the cave, the stone has been moved, which means all the heaviness that is life. He comes into a full awareness. So much God. We, too, when we emerge from the cave of our heart and the stone is moved, we come into our full awareness. So much God. Infinite. No borders, no boundaries. We see and we hear with all of our daily life. But there is something so much more. It is resurrection, His very presence. We come into our complete awareness. Before going into the cave of our heart, going into the great silence, we're just a small part of our awareness. So many thoughts, so many feelings, so busy. So much love and cruelty, so much of everything. So slowly, slowly, we follow the steps.

The first step is to surrender to our daily story. Don't push and pull it so much. And most importantly, don't judge. They do not know what they do. If we take back all judgment, we can just let go and be with our daily story. It's only a story. And no matter how difficult, how challenging, the cave of our heart awaits us. We breathe. There is a great silence here. There is a great nothing here. It's okay. Our awareness can let go of all the story. And in the cave of our heart, our awareness just relaxes. Unfolds. And spreads everywhere. In the beautiful silence of our heart, there is a stillness. We go deeper and deeper in the silence, and there's this peace. We go deeper, deeper in the peace, and we come to the very heart of our awareness. And inside this heart is another heart. In the cave of our heart, we find the heart inside our heart inside our heart, the great quiet. We breathe. And this quiet is our true heart. The light of our awareness. We breathe and drink this light. The daily world, the daily story, is very far away. Here there is only more, more, light. The light gets bigger and bigger and bigger, brighter! Our entire being is this light. Our awareness is one big smile of infinite light. It is in all our nerves. It is everywhere. And in this light is our true body. It has no beginning, no ending. In the cave of our heart, the darkness, the quiet, it just becomes light. So brilliant. So complete. Here there is no time. No effort. Only just being. We offer all that we are into the light. We offer our light into the greater light. It is everywhere. Inside of us, outside of us.

Holding us. We are held, the essence of love. There is nothing separate but light.

A special part of the story is when the stone is moved away and Christ appears outside of the cave, out of the great silence, the great nothing. Christ emerges and there's just so much light, it's so bright. The question is who are we when we emerge from the cave of our heart? How do we live? It's not so important that people see us or don't see us, what we do or don't do. We're beautiful as we breathe from the very heart of our awareness. We are living out of the very heart of our lives. Each person we live with, family and friends, their heart is also light. Even if they do not know their own resurrection. They're so busy, thinking, doing, working so hard. We can receive the very heart of everyone in our lives. We receive the heart, the nature, the ocean, the trees. We keep breathing in and out of the most-pure heart of our awareness. And our awareness keeps expanding bigger and bigger, so much light everywhere. This is life after resurrection. This is the beginning of the journey, not the end. The life after resurrection, who are we? How do we live? How much joy are we every day? This is the mystery. The beauty. The opportunity. We support each other in the big journey. We especially support each other in that life after we've discovered the very heart of our awareness, after we've found who we are in the great silence. We support each other after the stone has moved away.

Awakening, The Many Forms

There are many paths to the profound liberation of the soul.

Our awakening has many forms. On a mental level, it's giving up judgment. When we let go of judging ourselves and each other. When we let go of judging our daily story, judging all that is happening around us and in us, our awareness is no longer so tight. Our judgements are like a prison. They lock us into a certain point of view and keep us away from our awakening. When we let go of judging, our awareness walks out of our mental prison and is free. Suddenly we can see the heart that is always present. This is our mental awakening. To see and experience the heart that is always present, by letting go of all judgment. On an emotional level, our awakening is letting go of our regret for the past, and letting go of our worry about the future. Our regret and our worry locks our awareness and squeezes our true self. As we let go of regret and worry, we can be present. And the heart of life is always here. Present.

On a physical level, our awakening is not identifying so much with our body. We have good days and days that are not so good. Easy days and difficult days, our body is just the boat that we're riding. It's just the ship that we're on, the journey we are on. It's not who we are. As we let go of identifying so much with our body, the boat, we can enjoy the journey. As we let go of not identifying so much with all the needs and worries and repairs needed for the ship, we can just let go and be in the great pilgrimage of who we are.

Sooner or later, we're going to let go of this body, of our boat completely, and find another vessel. We find a much lighter vessel to travel in. Just our awareness, our hearts are present. On a more profound level, our awakening is this great, big space we find inside. It is so pure. So much light. So much brilliant light. In this space, we feel completely seen. We're just completely seen. And in these moments, we feel completely loved. Just totally loved. We are this love. And in this love, we feel completely safe. It's the safety beyond words, just so safe. And then we realize we've come home. This is our awakening.

Now some people experience this on a retreat or in a profound prayer. Some of us have had a near death experience where the mind is completely turned off and suddenly our awareness is totally present. In this great space is pure and endless love. There is no border, just more love. In these moments, we realize we are completely seen. We're safe and home. We can find our true awakening, our complete awakening, in the silence of our heart. This is our daily meditation. As we let go of judgment, regret, worry, identifying so much with our physical body, our physical life... we come into the silence of our heart. It's big, vast. In the silence of our heart, the knots in our awareness, they untangle. In the silence of our heart, our awareness is washed, everything is washed. As we come deeper and deeper into the silence of our heart, there is more, more space. Everything is washed and untangled. All of our personality dissolves.

There's more and more just nothing.…. emptiness. Silence. Emptiness is a great gift in the silence of our heart. Nothing to hold onto, nothing to do, nothing to think about. The great nothing, deeper and deeper emptiness, this emptiness is a bath for our soul. We keep coming deeper and deeper inside. There are no borders, no boundaries. As the emptiness unfolds into more, more emptiness… there is light. This light is our true awareness. In the beginning, it's very dim and far away. And slowly, slowly, in the profound emptiness, the light is everywhere. It is the light of who we are. We concentrate. We breathe into the very heart of our awareness. Inside our heart is another heart, and another heart. More, more, light. In this light we are completely seen. We are. Our awareness is so beautiful. There is so much love here. This light is complete love. Each of us are completely loved. No beginning, no ending, just love. As we receive this love, we realize we are love. Our awareness soaks in this. We just drink this, we breathe this. This is our meditation. So much light. So much love. We are completely safe here. We come home again. Every part of us is awakening. We are awake. We are home. We are this love.

Our awakening is not a one-time event. Something happens and we are forever awakened. Our awakening is a way of life. It's a path. It's a journey, a pilgrimage. Every day we practice letting go of our judgments about ourselves, each other, our daily story. The moment we let go of our judgments, our awareness walks out of the prison of so much thinking. Suddenly we're free. The heart of life is always here, it's always present. When we let go of our judgments, we see what is really present. So much beauty, so much heart. In all circumstances, no matter what is occurring inside and outside, our awareness is whole and complete. We let go of regrets about the past, worries about the future. Our awareness can breathe again. So much light, so much heart is here, now. And we don't identify so much with our bodies. These boats are just boats. Sometimes they're leaking, sometimes they're heavy, sometimes they're falling apart.

The boat has its journey but it's not who we are. As we don't identify so much with our body, we begin to realize the true body of our awareness, our hearts, the great love that is here. In our meditation we enjoy the silence. We go deeper and deeper into the silence of our heart. In the great emptiness, our busy mind, our thoughts, drifts away. In the great emptiness, our awareness unfolds into the big, big space of being. So much heart.

The light is here. And the love. We want to drink from the most-pure heart, the heart inside of our heart inside of another heart. This is our meditation. To drink as much love into every nerve of our body, every little tiny part of our awareness, until we are awakened into who we are. We discover our true purpose in these times. We're here to awaken. We just enjoy the heart of life, giving to the heart of life, celebrating the heart of life, ourselves, each other and the people we meet in every circumstance. Each of us find more, more purpose in the very heart of life as we awaken.

The Steps into Simple Peace

*Achieving simple peace, the soul's journey
of release into pure tranquility.*

The steps, the inner steps to more and more simple peace. You would think simple peace would be easy, it would be simple. For most of us it's not so simple. We're so busy in our daily world. So many desires. It's hard to find peace with so many desires. So many wants. It's hard to find simple peace when we want so much. We are so busy, and in our busyness it's hard to have simple peace. The spiritual journey is a whole other journey. It's a journey of letting go. And as we let go, we find some peace. It's a journey of letting be. As you practice to just be, you find some peace.

It's a journey of offering instead of wanting. It's a journey of really offering. And in our offering, slowly, slowly, we find more simple peace. We think things will get better when relationships change or work changes, or we make some change in the world. But normally what happens is that the story just changes. We don't really have simple peace. Underneath our daily story, all the things we carry in our awareness, there's an ocean of peace. As we practice letting go, letting be and offering, slowly, slowly, we unload all the stuff we carry in our awareness. Slowly, slowly, in our letting go, and in our offering, we let be, we find more and more peace.

The changes in our daily story may give us peace. But what really gives us peace is finding the space for peace inside. When we're so busy and carrying so much, there's no space for peace, even though it is all around us. It is at this moment. It is waiting for us. So as we slowly breathe and let go, offer everything that we're carrying inside, there is more and more space. And this is the second big step in simple peace. First is letting go of our daily story and business. The second step is finding more and more space inside. This is our source of peace. We come deeper and deeper inside, and there's a vastness, an emptiness, more space for simple peace. As we breathe and receive the peace of this moment, we come deeper and deeper into our heart. This is the third step, the source of simple peace. As we receive the simple heart inside, the presence of our own heart, the gentleness, as we let go of all the busyness and the thoughts and judgments, the peace of our heart comes more and more forward. We come deeper into the source of our simple peace, which is the pure heart inside our heart. As we find more space in our heart, we find more of the very heart of our awareness. The peace inside spreads, inside and everywhere. We keep offering, letting go of thoughts, anything we're carrying. And with the in breath, we come deeper and deeper into the heart of our heart, into the heart of our awareness.

We receive the gentleness, the stillness, the pure quiet, the openness. We fall into the great peace inside. We let go and fall into more and more peace. This is who we really are. Our awareness gets bigger and bigger and spreads. It has no beginning, no ending. In this great peace inside, there is no time. We just are. We keep letting go and fall deeper and deeper into the peace of our own essence. This is our true body, a body of peace. It's in our bones and our nerves. It's everywhere. As we enter this realm of peace, the noise of the world, the noise of our daily life falls further and further away. The peace is so much greater. The opportunity is to go inside this peace. We see the peace inside the peace. There's no words here. There's lightness and being.

We breathe and see as much light of our original peace as we can. We are innocent here. We are home. The peace of our inner heart fills every room inside. Every place inside is filled with more peace. This is our meditation. Every corner of our being is peace. And we want to receive this peace. Absorb all the peace. We just are.

The Inner Steps to Expanded Awareness

The three steps to expanded awareness show us how to be free of constricted awareness and enjoy our awakened self. Listening deeply, receiving the qualities of our inner heart, embracing emptiness together lead us into an inner vastness, our expanded awareness.

We meditate on the inner steps to expand awareness. Most of us live in what we call constricted awareness. So much thinking, feeling, doing, our awareness is caught in all the ups and downs of daily life, all the challenges. In truth, our awareness is the size of a great big sea of awareness, an ocean of beingness. But it gets squeezed into constricted awareness. We think it's normal to be thinking all the time. But it's just a habit. When we live in constricted awareness, there's a feeling of never having enough. We always want more. Life must be bigger, larger, no matter how much we have. It's not enough. We think the problem is work, or relationships, or love, or our home, but really the problem is we live in constricted awareness. We have moments of peace. But in expanded awareness, we have more than moments. There is a great big expansion of peace.

There are three secrets to expanded awareness. The first, when we go into silence, meditation, when we make a silent retreat, it's all about listening. It's not so much about not talking, it's about listening. As we begin to listen deeply, the mind begins to calm down, not so many thoughts. As we listen more deeply, the thoughts get more in the distance. We begin to hear something special, awareness itself. Listening creates space inside. And in this space, we find our expanded awareness. We're not constricted into worrying and thinking and wanting so many things. As we listen, we find more and more space inside. Our awareness becomes expanded. The peace, instead of being squeezed into moments, has no beginning, no ending. There's a vastness of peace inside of us.

The second secret to expanded awareness, after we begin listening inside, is to receive as deeply as we can the presence of our own heart. You cannot listen and think at the same time. Similarly, you can't be receiving and thinking at the same time. So as we go deeper and receive the softness, the peace within, the quiet of our own heart, our busy mind becomes even less. As we go deeper into expanded awareness, the great quiet of our own heart grows in our awareness. As we receive, we can listen even more deeply. There's more space. As we listen, we can go even further into the heart inside our heart. We can receive more the pure presence of being, the great stillness within, the love, the gentleness, the kindness in our own heart. As we receive the qualities of our heart, the mind gets less and less. All of our concerns, all of our challenges get smaller and smaller. It is the qualities of our own heart. Kindness. Gentleness. Love. Peacefulness. This is our source of healing. It's our source of expanded awareness. As we listen deeply, as we receive the qualities of our heart, here, there is enough. The search, the grasping, is over. We keep going deeper inside, and we find this place with no beginning, no ending. This is expanded awareness, our abundant self.

The third secret to expanded awareness, after listening deeply, receiving the qualities of our own heart, is to embrace emptiness. It's out of habit we keep trying to fill up our lives, fill our minds, be busy, keep filling things up. But this keeps us in constricted awareness. As we let go into a big emptiness inside, here our awareness continues spreading and spreading. We welcome emptiness. It's not really empty, it's just awareness. The qualities of our heart come forward. The pure peacefulness. The quiet, kindness, and gentleness, the qualities of our heart grow as we embrace emptiness. How do we embrace emptiness? We keep offering everything in our awareness. We offer, keep letting go, and offering. Then we can listen even again, more deeply. We can receive, again, even more of the true substance of our heart. And finally emptiness becomes a great friend. With emptiness there's no border between us and life itself. Expanded awareness and we're really fully present. The moment is so much. To be fully present is to have more than enough. It's to find beauty in the smallest things. Grace. Expanded awareness is our true being, our true awareness.

There are times to think, but there's also times to just be. We keep listening deeply, receiving the pure heart inside our heart, and welcoming emptiness. Here there's just more and more beingness. There is no time. We just are. Slowly, slowly, this is not just a meditation. There's a way of life, to live in expanded awareness. We live in this great being inside. We discover it everywhere. We discover more and more presence. Listening, receiving, emptying, life itself is in our hands and heart. It's everywhere.

The three secrets to expanded awareness. We practice listening. As we listen more deeply, we hear what is behind the words, what is underneath the noise. We begin hearing a pulse of awareness, the pulse of life itself. As our awareness rests and listens inside, it spreads and expands. We hear a great OM in silence. We hear the wordless words of life itself. And as we practice receiving the qualities of our own heart, gentleness, life, peacefulness, joy, our awareness becomes more full of its true nature. We expand in gentleness, peacefulness, light. The qualities of our heart frees us of the knots, the stress. The qualities of our heart naturally expands our awareness into the great ocean.

As our awareness is expanding, we get out of the habit of wanting and filling things up, trying so hard to make something happen. We welcome emptiness. In emptiness our awareness spreads deeper in all directions. It just spreads. Ironically, in emptiness, we really have enough. We find the presence of peace, of life itself. Instead of living in constricted awareness, we're invited to live an expanded being, expanded awareness. Here we begin to make new choices. More simplicity, more listening, more receiving, the beauty itself is here as we receive the qualities of our heart.

Life After Our Awakening

What do you do after having an earth-shattering spiritual revelation?

What is the best path for us, after we've had our spiritual awakening? There are many paths to awakening. Some people experience it when in retreat, a life changing experience, a dream, prayer. There are many paths into our essence. In the nakedness of the moment, when we just are, letting go, we find ourselves. We are in a big realm of peace. As we experience this peace, we feel God is totally present. God sees every part of us, every hair on our body. There is a beautiful oneness. We have this deep communion with all, the universe, whatever we call it.

Some people find awakening in their meditation. As they go inside, their mind becomes less busy... and slowly, slowly, it's just... not there at all. They go into the silence of their heart. Here is everything. They go deeper into the everything. And they find their true nature, their true self. So much love is present. So much peace.

Some people go into awakening in a near-death experience. Suddenly, the mind is gone. It's dead. And yet, here is awareness, and this awareness goes forever. Everyone and everything is connected. And the love is beyond words. The colors are beyond color. The sounds, everything, is something really beyond what we normally know. There's so much life, in its own way. So much love.

The Christians, all the Christian religions, find awakening each in their own way. They come to this light, this Christ-light, and it gets bigger and bigger inside of them, and soon they discover that Christ is absorbing them. As they let go into the Christ-light, Christ totally absorbs us. There is nothing but Christ, nothing but this light. The Buddhists find their Buddha nature, which is their heart wisdom, which is a peace beyond words. The Hindus and their offering and their humility and their devotion, all the different gods and goddesses pick up a different part of their heart and hold their awareness. In a special beauty, in a very deep, old tradition of love. All religions lead us within to the heart within our heart.

Some people find their awakening in a crisis, when suddenly everything is naked. Someone's dying, or there's an illness or an accident, and suddenly the story goes away and there's nothing—there's only just the present moment and this present moment is totally naked, and in this nakedness, they discover something else. Their awareness is awakened to how much God is present, in the nakedness of this moment. Angels can appear, loved ones can appear, love in any form can suddenly be present. And in this naked moment, they are totally changed.

And in some cultures, particularly Native cultures, people grow up in awakening. In Bali, the babies are held for the first six months. They do not touch the ground. Imagine being held for the first six months. So the Balinese are held and slowly wake up in this love. And they keep waking up in this love. And all their spiritual traditions add to this love leaving the people so beautiful, so gentle, so open. Their awareness is expanded in this love.

Our awakening, whether it was five months ago or twenty years ago, whether it was just a few minutes or a few hours or a few days, it is so real. More real than real. And it never leaves us. It stays in us. It's more than a memory, more than a dream, more than an event. The love is so complete. It is always with us. On the other hand, we live in a culture, particularly our modern culture, that doesn't support our awakening. So daily life veils, pushes away this experience. In the awakening, everything is so simple, so present, so true. And our daily life can be so complicated, difficult, challenging. In our awakening there is no worry. Just endless freedom and our awareness becomes so free. It just keeps becoming more free, more and more free. And in our daily life there is so much reason to worry, competition. We judge ourselves. We judge each other. Meanwhile our awakening is only forgiveness. The love is so pure. It's more than forgiveness. It's more than innocence. It's an endless beingness.

The challenge is not to have our awakening just in a little corner inside, or a small room inside. The opportunity is to have our awakening more with us every day. We live in the world, but not of the world. Our awakening can grow and grow. We can take the opportunity to embrace and receive our awakening, to let it grow. In our everyday life, our awareness becomes constricted. So busy, so much thinking, so much feeling, so much doing. In our awakening, our awareness just keeps spreading and spreading forever. Everyone and everything is included. The intimacy is beyond words.

So our meditation is to maintain, to continue awakening in daily life. Every day we take time, we don't hold our daily story so tightly. We remember this place of no time. No story, we let go of our busy thoughts, everything we have to do, everything that's on our mind. We practice letting go of all this. We remember our awakening—no thought, no mind, nothing to do. Life itself is present. In our noisy world, we travel, journey into the silence of our own heart. The silence washes our busy mind, washing all of our thoughts. The silence washes our daily story. We go more into the silence of our heart. The silence is very pure here. Our habits, our patterns are being washed. It's just a habit to think so much. It's a habit to be reactive and defensive and to worry. All these things are habits. In the deep silence of our heart, these patterns untangle. The habits are washed. We remember our awakening, our true self, our true nature. As we go further into the heart inside our heart, we discover the very heart of our awareness. This is the home we find in our awakening. We want to remember this home inside. We are completely safe here. We are completely seen. There is only love inside and outside. As we travel into the heart of our heart, inside the pure heart inside, our awareness is as a little ball of pure light. But this ball opens and opens and spreads everywhere. It has no beginning, no ending. We breathe. Just more, more brilliant light, it's so bright, it's so much.

In the daily world, there is a feeling of not having enough. Here we remember there is enough. There is more than enough. We receive the abundance of who we are. And it's so beautiful. As we go into the center of our center, we discover the very center of the universe is inside of us, all the planets and the stars. We are so whole. Everything fits together. There are no mistakes. In the center of our center, the universe, everything is okay. All is held. We breathe. Our entire nervous system is on fire with light. Joy. Peace. Our nervous system extends to everyone. Everything. We all share the nervous system of the universe. It's all perfect. We concentrate on receiving the most-pure heart deep inside our heart. Here, our awakening is happy, free, more peaceful than peaceful, more love than love.

Whether our awakening was just one experience of a few minutes, a few hours, or a few days, or it comes many times through the years. Our awakening is a gift. These are seeds that are planted in the garden of our life. We want to spend time with these seeds and let them grow through our entire being into every part of our life. We want to give more of our awareness to our awakening. We are free here. We want to shine our hearts upon these seeds. We give our hearts to this awakening. Our life has more sunshine, more love. We want to let the garden grow inside, outside. The garden of our awakening grows everywhere. This is our purpose. This is who we are.

There are three parts of life after our awakening. The first is our spiritual practice. Every day, we want to go into the great silence of our own heart... and absorb all the peace that is present here. We want to make retreat, whether it's a few days, or much longer. We give ourselves a gift from the complicated world to the simplicity of retreat. Be in the joy of retreat. The presence of our own awakening. The second part is community. We want to be in community that supports us, and we support each other. We support each other in a complicated world. And we do this just by receiving each other deeply. Community, each one of us, is such a gift, so unique, so precious. The garden is totally special and beautiful and unique in each of us. Community is very important. And the third part after our awakening is our service. We give our hearts into the world. This can just be a smile or a helping hand, or it can be a project. It doesn't matter how big or small it is. As we pour our hearts into the world, our awakening grows. We realize how much is being poured in us, and through us. Our awakeness is borderless, endless, the love has no beginning, no ending. Our purpose is through our service. Moment to moment, day by day, may we find more, more beauty every day.

Emptying The Busy Mind

Constant thinking is only a habit. When we learn to empty our busy mind, we can find true peace.

Meditation is to empty the busy mind. We are so busy in our minds. Many people, when they meditate, they think about not thinking. And then after 20 minutes they're so frustrated thinking about not thinking. Other people, when they meditate, they have a mantra or a few words. But around the mantra are so many busy thoughts and so much of a busy mind. As soon as the mantra stops, the busy mind goes again. Some people, when they meditate, they watch all their thoughts and all their feelings. And they keep watching so many thoughts and so many feelings. And after 20 minutes they think, "Wow, it's never going to stop, so many thoughts and so many feelings." And they have a little peace in the meditation. But the busy mind is still there. The key to stopping the busy mind is emptiness.

In our culture we don't talk about emptiness too much. When the glass is half empty, we're always ready to fill it up. We're so focused on filling up the cup, we never take time for the cup being half empty or empty. So our mind is always working, busy, busy. There's this feeling that there's never enough. Not enough money, not enough space, not enough friends, not enough work, not enough, we're always working on "there's not enough."

Winter is an important time of year, just to become still, quiet, empty. Many of you know that we take groups to Bali every year. In Bali, the prayer begins with remembering emptiness. And then they begin offering everything in their heart to God and all the forms of God. Many of you know that we lived in Assisi, Italy, the home of St. Francis, for many years. St Francis would go up to his cave on top of the hill and sit with Lady Poverty, which was emptiness. Emptiness is not about being poor and suffering and giving up everything. Emptiness is an inner reality of being quiet. St. Francis called emptiness Lady Poverty. And she's beautiful. When you get to know winter, when you get to know emptiness, it's very, very beautiful. The first Mystics would go into the desert, not to suffer for God, but to experience the emptiness, where our awareness is not so busy, where we just are our awareness. A whole other world opens up. So we invite everyone, all of us, to appreciate emptiness. It's in everyone's life. Everyone has some place that is empty, where there's not enough. Maybe our house is not enough, our partner is not enough, our work is not enough, our health is not enough. This emptiness, like winter, is part of life, it's everywhere. It's in all of us.

Instead of trying to rush into spring and summer, the mystics in all religions, they stay with winter, with emptiness. When our awareness empties out of all the busyness, we just have our awareness. The journey begins here. We let go of our daily story, we don't hold it so tightly. It's just a story. Every page, every chapter, moves and changes. When we don't hold our story tightly, our mental busyness is less and less. As we offer and let go, the emptiness, from being little, gets bigger and bigger, like winter, like a field of snow, white and quiet. What happens when we embrace emptiness is that we come into the silence of our own heart. And the silence is beautiful. We come deeper inside, into the pure quiet of our own heart. Here, there is no mental world. There is quiet, stillness. Our meditation begins here. It is this pure quiet that calls the mystics in all religions. As we go deeper into the heart inside our heart, our awareness spreads. Here, there's a vastness. Emptiness is beautiful with more and more space inside. As we come into the heart inside our heart and breathe, here, there is enough.

There is so much heart inside our heart. Winter is very beautiful. The peace inside the quiet, and inside this peace is another peace. We want to receive the pure heart inside our heart. And as the emptiness spreads and spreads and gets bigger and bigger inside, this peace becomes more pure, more peaceful. We breathe. This piece spreads everywhere, inside and outside. So much emptiness, so much quiet, so much peace. We concentrate to receive the very heart of our awareness. It is a big emptiness. All the planets and stars are inside of us. So much space, so much being, we come into the very center of our center. Here, there is no story. We just are. And as we come deeper into the center of our center, there is more, more light. We drink this light. It is everywhere. Inside of us, outside of us. This is the pure light of winter. But it's not cold, it's warm. It holds us, it is us. It is our true awareness. The very heart of our awareness is who we are. And the great emptiness, the heart inside our heart, is so present. We just want to be here. The heart is inside of us, all around us. it is inside everything and everyone, more, more heart.

When we welcome emptiness, our busy mind gets less. In the emptiness, there is a doorway to the great silence. And in the great silence, we find our heart. The very heart of our awareness. The silence washes our awareness. The silence untangles the knots. It gently blows away the fears. We let go of all our frustration. In the silence of our heart, the emptiness opens to a big vastness of peace. We breathe.

There is a place in all of us that is not enough. This is part of being a human. There's not enough money, not enough love, not enough work, we miss our loved ones. This feeling of not enough is an opportunity. Emptiness empties all the frustration, all the mental energy. Emptiness brings us into the great silence inside. And out of winter comes a spring like we never knew. It's a completely different spring. It's magical. It's the spring that comes out of the heart inside our heart. It is Awakening. There's no words for it. It's incredible. This is why the mystics in all religions went into emptiness, the desert, the cave. Because in the quiet of the heart, there is everything. There is so much. The jewels and the diamonds and the treasure of life. We support each other, we are all doing the best we can. Let us realize being human is beautiful. Being human means that we all have an empty place somewhere in our lives. This emptiness is an opportunity to hold the golden heart inside of us, and we find the golden heart inside of us, we see it in each of us, we see it in everyone, life becomes more golden. It's very beautiful.

Opening to Our Soft Awareness

*In our daily lives it is difficult to be open, spontaneous,
and whimsical. Nurturing one's inner child opens
the gates to living a happy and fulfilling life.*

How do we soften our awareness? With so much thinking and so
much doing, our awareness becomes constricted. We become a
little bit hard and tough. Soft awareness is gentle, innocent, wide,
open. With all the pressures in the world and stress that everybody
is working with, our awareness is complicated, our mind stays busy.
And we think this is normal. But it's just a habit to have a busy
mind. It's just a habit to be thinking all the time. Our awareness
can be soft, not so busy. We don't need to be thinking all the time.
We can be more inside, living gently in our inner self of just being.

So how do we develop soft awareness? You want to spend more
time with little children. babies. Just feel their awareness as a path
to remembering our original awareness. Gentle, soft, spontaneous.
We want to spend time with the little child in each of us. Then
with friends, family, partners, feel the presence of the people in
our lives. It's not important how much we say to each other, what
we do with each other. What is beautiful is to receive each other,
receiving each person's unique presence in our lives. This gives
us soft awareness. We all have personalities. Sometimes it's easy.
Sometimes more difficult. They're just personalities. We want to

spend time with the being of the people in our lives, and receive their unique beingness. Everyone touches us differently. Everyone is a gift. Their presence in our lives nourishes our soft awareness. We want to spend more time in nature, less time absorbed in thinking, doing. Every day is the practice of receiving our inner softness, our beingness.

Underneath our busy mind there's the river of our awareness. We can call this river the Ganges inside each of us. We can call it the Sacred River. Whatever we call the river that runs inside all of us, it connects us to the ocean. A great ocean of being, of light, of love. So as we come underneath our busy mind, we come to the river of our awareness, the Ganges running through each of us. And the river of our awareness connects all of us. We are more connected than we know. Wherever we are, we're in the soft awareness. Whenever we're in the river of our awareness, we are connected in the great ocean. In this ocean, we are held. We are safe. We are loved. We are love. Each of us is called to remember who we are. This is our purpose, to come underneath the busy mind and to the great heart inside of us. Here, everything is very soft. Very giving. Here, everything is very whole.

The key for coming into the river of our awareness, to the Ganges inside of us, is silence. The silence washes our busy minds. Silence untangles our complicated life, our worries, and doubts. The silence restores us to our true awareness which is very, very, soft and whole. We receive the silence every day, every moment. The silence in each other, that's the presence. The silence in nature, the quiet is always here, washing our awareness. Restoring our awareness, in the great silence we receive, we come deeper inside. In the great silence, there's more, more softness. Safety. Freedom.

As we come deeper into the softness, it gets bigger. It has no borders, no boundaries. Our awareness has no borders, it just expands, inside, outside. It extends everywhere. As we come to the softness of who we are, there is more and more light because this is the very heart of our awareness. This is our concentration. To receive the heart of each moment, the heart of the people we are with, the heart of nature, The heartfulness, this presence is our home, connecting us truly to everyone. Inside our heart is another heart. It is more soft. We can breathe here. As we come deeper into the heart inside our heart, there's a whole universe of light. Openness. We're coming home. This home is very special. We're coming to the very center of our center which is the center of who we are, of the whole universe. So soft, open, giving, whole, sweet, we breathe. We feel the center of all the planets and the stars inside of us, everywhere. The heart inside of our heart is our source of healing, of well-being. The heart of our awareness is so pure, true. Everything is good here.

There is light. Our awareness is soft again. We receive the softness through our whole being. We feel the softness inside everyone. In nature, in our homes. It is the river running underneath the busy minds, the river bringing us to the ocean. Softness. Beauty. Peace. Joy. The key to softness is to receive. To be.

As we come into the softness of our own heart, we can breathe. We come deeper and deeper into the river of our awareness. This is the Ganges, a sacred river, running through all of us. There's a story about the Ganges, when the pilgrims go into the Ganges and wash and bathe, the tourists look at the pilgrims and say, how can you go in that river? It's so dirty. And the pilgrims smile. They say, "The river, the Ganges is not dirty, it's the dirt that's dirty." It's the same when we come into the river of our awareness. There are so many things in it, so much stuff. But our awareness is not dirty, it's the stuff, it's all the things we carry in our awareness.

To the river of our awareness, coming into the Ganges inside all of us, we stand in the very heart of our awareness, the very heart of the river. We offer everything. And then when we breathe in we receive everything. All the softness. All the heart that's present. And then when we exhale again, we offer everything, all the stuff, all the things. And then we inhale into our inner awareness, into our heart, into the Ganges. And we find freedom. Complete freedom. Freedom into our awareness is an ocean of just love. We're all connected here. We hold each other, we support each other, we are one here. May we all enjoy more and more softness in this life. And may it grow into little flowers, simple joy, more peace inside, and everywhere.

The Three Jewels of Spirituality

Three tenets across all traditions of spirituality:
silence, emptiness, and devotion.

These Jewels are in all traditions. Each Jewel is a gift. We want to open this gift, sit with it, be with it, live with it. As we open and receive these gifts, the three Jewels of spirituality, the gift has no ending. It just keeps giving, giving, and giving. We want these Jewels to be the cornerstone of our lives, the cornerstone of the temple inside of us all, in everything. I've discovered these Jewels in little pieces and different parts of the world. I'm just beginning to realize how beautiful, how important they are. So I invite you to receive these Jewels, hold them, sit with them, breathe, and live with them. They free us completely. It's a gift without end, each of these Jewels.

The first Jewel of spirituality is silence. We spend so much time talking and thinking. This talking and thinking, all this mental busyness is like a filter. It's like a blanket. It covers the real, true reality of Who We Are. Silence is a Jewel that we can open again and again. We begin to see. We begin to really understand. Most people live in the busyness of their mental worlds. This is like the waves on the ocean. They spend their entire life trying to be comfortable but the waves on the ocean are just the very surface of our awareness. Underneath the waves is an ocean of silence.

When we live on the waves of the ocean, being busy trying to be comfortable, there's a feeling that there's never enough. No matter how much we have, how much we do, the waves keep bouncing us around. But underneath the waves is an ocean of Silence. The ocean of our awareness. Here, there is enough. There is more than enough.

Every day we want to remember Each person in our lives is a unique presence of Silence. Each of our children, they're a gift of sacred silence. Each one is a different flavor of Silence, a different presence of Silence. When we live in the ocean of silence, when we live in our true awareness, silence is beautiful. It is always holding us, giving to us, being with us. To live on the surface of our awareness, thinking and talking, is to miss who we really are. The ocean of our awareness is deep, quiet, precious. The Jewel of spirituality of silence is an opportunity to soak. We want to be like a sponge every day, soak in the Silence of our awareness. soak in the Silence of the people we are with, soak in the Silence that is everywhere. Just like a sponge, we want to breathe in silence, exhale silence. We discover the awareness deep, deep inside, that has no ending, no beginning. In the silence, we are connected to everything and everyone. There's no fear. In the silence, we are completely safe. we find our home inside.

The second Jewel of spirituality is emptiness. Most people are afraid of emptiness. They keep trying to fill it up, to change it. But there's always a place in life that is empty. It's okay. It's a reminder. We may not have enough work, not enough money. We may be lonely, without good health. Emptiness shows up in many parts of our lives. It's part of being human. Emptiness is a Jewel of spirituality. It's a gift. Instead of fighting emptiness, struggling with emptiness, we go deep inside into emptiness. Here is more silence. It's a doorway into the divine, into presence. Emptiness is not the end of the journey. It's actually the beginning of the journey. Without emptiness, our mind is just busy. There's no room for the divine, for our awareness.

So every day we welcome emptiness. We go through the doorway into the space of emptiness, we discover more and more space, vastness within. There's a whole universe of emptiness inside each of us. Emptiness is our friend. Saint Francis used to call emptiness Lady Poverty. He loved her because he realized Lady Poverty, Lady Emptiness, brings you into the whole universe. The whole world into the great silence. Our heart can be filled with so many things, and emptiness unloads us. We come into the true depths of our heart. And that's what we want. In our heart there's silence. And as we go deeper into silence, there's more and more emptiness, more and more space. As we go deeper into the space, into this vastness, we discover the planets and the Stars inside of us. We discover the very heart of our awareness. We don't want to live apart from our heart. We don't want to live on the waves of our ocean. We want to live in the very heart of our ocean. The very heart of our awareness. The Jewel of emptiness brings us deeper into the heart of who we are, our essence. We find the essence of life everywhere. Emptiness is such a gift. May this beautiful space inside open everywhere. In emptiness we are connected to each other and everyone.

The third Jewel of spirituality is essential, very special. This is the Jewel of devotion. Once we find this big space inside, the silence, the emptiness, we want to grow our true heart back into our awareness. In our culture, upbringing, all the noise we live with, our heart gets squeezed smaller and smaller. Spirituality is actually growing heart, nothing more, nothing less. The most direct way of growing heart is the Jewel of devotion. This means when we end the silence and the emptiness, we want to offer everything in our heart into the divine.

Everything in our heart, we offer. We let it go. We offer it to the one God everywhere. As we offer, then the heart gets bigger. First, we offer a small cup of our love, and then we find a bowl of love. Then we offer the bowl of love, and we find a really great big bowl of love. Then we offer that and we find a whole pond of love. We keep offering and we find a lake of love. Pretty soon we keep offering and offering everything in our heart, and we find the ocean. We find the ocean of silence, the ocean of emptiness, is actually love. We discover this through devotion through offering. So in our meditation we offer everything to the one God. We offer everything in our heart to all the manifestations of God. We offer everything in our heart to our loved ones and ancestors on the other side. We offer everything into our heart. And slowly become deeper into the heart of who we are. We concentrate. We receive the pure heart inside our heart, and we offer this. Our awareness finds more heart, more light. We offer this. We keep going deeper into the silence of who we are, into the great emptiness, the heart is inside of us. The heart is everywhere. We offer this in the in-breath. We go deeper into the heart. It is everywhere. On the out-breath we offer everything, we let it go and offer it. So much love.

So much light. So brilliant, so bright. It spreads and spreads and we keep offering. We breathe.

These three Jewels, they work together. As we open one gift, we can open the next and the next more deeply and receive it more. We want to open the gift of silence again and again. As we go deep into silence, the waves of daily life don't touch us so much because we are living in the ocean of our awareness. The ocean of silence underneath the busy waves, as we come deeper into the silence of our awareness, we discover the joy of emptiness. In the joy of emptiness, the waves of daily life, all the busyness and noise, is further and further away. In emptiness, we discover what Saint Francis calls Lady Poverty. She is beautiful. She is within nature, our partner, our friends. She is everywhere. In emptiness, we are one community. We are all naked. We discover this vast space inside, this big emptiness, the very heart of our awareness comes more forward.

It is devotion that expresses the heart. And as we express the heart we find more. We offer our little heart and it becomes bigger. We offer our bigger heart and it becomes really big. Then we keep offering our heart and we discover the very ocean of heart inside each of us. People ask, what should I do with my life? Why am I here? What is this all about? It's simple. Silence, emptiness, and the most importantly, devotion. We offer our heart every day when we meet somebody at the store, our friends, our family, our work. Wherever we are, we offer the pure heart inside of us. It doesn't matter the form, what is beautiful is the pure heart of our devotion, bringing it into the world.

As we find more silence, emptiness, our heart grows. We discover the heart is everywhere. We all share the same heart. It's beautiful that we can sit together in one heart, just being in silence. Emptiness, devotion, may our inner temple grow in these beautiful Jewels. May we shine everywhere, brilliantly shine, and everyone be happy, lots and lots of simple joys.

The Path to The Great Peace, The Peace Within Peace

The great peace is in the heart within our heart.
The great peace is light, unending, our essence,
the peace within us, everyone, everything.

We all have moments of peace. Maybe an afternoon or a day of peace. But the great peace is something else. There's really something beyond words, there are no words. It's a peace inside and outside, all around us, just unending peace. Inside peace is another peace, and this is the great peace. This peace that is inside peace, it's really light. It's really a great light. It is our own light, unending light.

The key to the path of the great peace begins with space. The peace is already here, but we have to make space for it to really receive and enjoy it. We need space in our daily life. We are so busy doing all the time that a few minutes of not doing is not enough. We need really to take an hour every day and not do and just be. When we learn how to do nothing, when we learn how to be nothing, Suddenly, there is everything. In the nothing, and the not doing, we discover so much everything. So much peace. So every day we want to take time to not be doing, but just to be. You want to make retreats. We want to learn how to be nothing so we become aware of everything. This is the great peace.

And then on the inside, again the magic word, the secret, is space. Most of us have no space. Our mind is so busy thinking, feeling, doing. Every day we want to have space outside and inside. And you come deeper and deeper in this space inside. You find more, more space. Here is the peace in the space inside. We let go and offer all of our busyness. Our thinking is just a habit, to be thinking all the time. We want to come to this space of nothing. So much space, so much vastness, so much being, this vastness inside… this is the home of the great silence. The silence inside of silence. So the key to the path of the great silence is space, outside and inside. We come deeper and deeper inside, into the Silence of our heart. And here is a peace. We come deeper and deeper inside to this big space. And here is more and more simple being, peace. We breathe. We keep coming deeper into more space, vastness. It has no beginning, no ending. Space is the path to the great peace, the peace inside of peace.

As we begin finding more, more space, the next keyword is to receive. You don't want to just sit in this space. You don't want to just watch the space. You want to receive this space, be this peace. We receive in every nerve of our being. The trees are receiving space. The people in our lives are space. The nature is receiving this peace. This peace is everywhere and everything. We feel the whole world, inside and outside, as a sponge for peace. We soak in peace. With each breath we receive more. The great peace is everywhere. As we come into the heart inside our heart, here is the home of the great peace. Here is our original light, our original awareness. We come deeper and deeper inside into the very heart of our awareness. So much space. We receive this space, this heart. The peace in our heart inside our heart gets bigger and bigger, it spreads everywhere. Deep inside in the center of our center, there is the light of the great peace.

We go to the light and the light comes to us. More, more peace, more, more light. It gets brighter, bigger. We are in the very center of our center. The great peace is everywhere. The light is so bright, so big it has no beginning, no ending. This peace is our true body. This light is our true awareness. With each breath, we are this peace, this light. We just be. Here, there is no time. Only presence. Peace, light.

The path to the great peace, the peace that is inside of peace, becomes clear. And in daily life as we find space for peace, when we have time for peace, not to be so busy doing all the time, but just being. In doing nothing we find everything. We find the great peace. The path to the great peace becomes clear in our inner life. As we find more space, the key is space in our daily life, space in our inner life. As we find more space inside, the very heart, the very essence of who we are, comes forward. The path to the great peace is through our heart. Through the heart of our teachers, into the heart of God, so much peace here. God is everywhere in everyone and everything. As we find more space, we find more peace. So much light, so much peace. We just breathe and soak in the peace that is everywhere, that is home in our own hearts.

We are all on the path to the great peace together. We are all instruments of peace. We want to be anchors of simple peace in daily life. This is our gift to the world. To be anchors of simple peace. It's in everything that we do, everything that we are. It's in your beautiful smile, your beautiful heart. It's our purpose to be anchors of this beautiful peace.

Infinite Heart Awareness

The path of a heart centered life.

We all have moments of peace. Maybe an afternoon or a day of peace. But great peace is something else. There's really something beyond words, there are no words. This is a peace inside and outside, all around us. It's just unending peace. Inside peace is another peace, and this is the great peace. This peace that is inside peace, it's really light, it's really a great light. It is our own light. Unending light.

The key to the path of the great peace begins with space. The peace is already here, but we have to make space for it to really receive and enjoy it. We need space in our daily life. We are so busy doing all the time that a few minutes of not doing is not enough. We need to really take an hour every day and not do, and just be. When we learn how to do nothing, when we learn how to be nothing, suddenly there is everything. In the nothing and the not doing, we discover so much. Everything, so much peace. So every day we want to take time to not be doing, but just to be. We want to make retreats. We're going to learn how to be nothing so we become aware of everything. And this is a great peace. And then on the inside, again the magic word, the secret, is space. Most of us have no space. Our mind is so busy thinking, feeling, doing. Every day we want to have space outside and inside. And as you come deeper and deeper in this space inside, you find more and more space. Here is the peace and the space inside. We let go and offer all of our busyness. Our thinking is just a habit, to be thinking all the time. We want to come to this space of nothing. So much space, so much vastness, so much being. This vastness inside… this is the home of the great silence, the silence inside of silence. So the key to the path to the great silence of space, outside and inside, we come deeper and deeper inside, into the silence of our heart, and here is the peace. We come deeper inside to this big space, and here's more and more. Being. Peace. We breathe. We keep coming deeper and deeper into more and more space, vastness. It has no beginning, no ending. This space is the path to great peace, the peace inside of peace.

As we begin finding more and more space, the next key word is to receive. You don't want to just sit in the space, you don't want to just watch a space, you want to breathe and receive this space, this peace. Receive in every nerve of our being. The trees are receiving space. The people in our lives, our space. Nature is receiving this peace. This peace is everywhere, in everything. We feel the whole world, inside and outside, as a sponge for peace. We soak in peace. With each breath, we receive more and more.

The great peace… is everywhere. As we come into the heart deep inside our heart, here is the home of the great peace. Here is our original light. Our original awareness. We come deeper and deeper inside, into the very heart of our awareness. So much space. We receive the space, this heart. The peace and the heart inside our heart gets bigger and bigger, it spreads everywhere. Deep inside, in the center of our center, there is the light of the great peace. We go to the light, and the light comes to us. More and more peace, more, more light. It gets brighter and brighter, bigger and bigger. We're in the very center of our center. Great peace is everywhere. The light is so bright, so big, no beginning, no ending. This peace is our true body. This light is our true awareness. With each breath... we are this peace, this light. We simply are. Here, there is no time. All is presence, peace, light.

The path to great peace, the peace that is inside of peace. It becomes clear in daily life as we find space for peace, when I have time for peace, not to be so busy doing all the time, but just being. And doing nothing, we find everything. We find the great peace. The path to great peace becomes clear in our inner life as we find more and more space. The key is space in daily life, space in our inner life. As we find more and more space inside, the very heart, the very essence of who we are comes forward. The path of great peace is through our heart. Through the heart of our teachers, into the heart of God. So much peace here. God is everywhere, and everyone, and everything. As we find more and more space, we find more and more peace. So much light. So much peace. We just breathe and soak in the peace. That is everywhere.

That is who we are. That is home in our own hearts. We're all on the path to great peace together. We're all instruments of peace. We want to be anchors of simple peace in daily life. This is our gift to the world, to be anchors of simple peace. It's in everything that we do, everything that we are, it's in your beautiful smiles and your beautiful heart. It's our purpose to be anchors of this beautiful peace.

The Keys to Our Awakening, The Pilgrimage Within

Our awakening is not complicated. If we follow a few keys, we step out of daily time into timelessness and the pilgrimage within. Eternity awaits us here.

The first key is to take the time. When we step out of daily time, we come into these timeless moments, where there is no time. In these timeless moments, we awaken to what is really present. We awaken to our own essence, the essence of life that is all around and within us. So it's important that we step out of our daily time, that we have our daily meditation practice, time in nature, free time, time for silence. And when we step out of daily time, we come into the real time, which are timeless moments, the timeless reality. The moment we step into timelessness, we begin finding another space. Outside and inside, this space is the space for our awakening. The space for our inner journey, our pilgrimage. Most people, they have no space. Their minds are busy. Their life is busy. Everything is busy inside and around them. When there's no space, we have moments of awakening, but they come and they go. As we step into timelessness, we find more space, outside, and most important, inside. We breathe. There is an endless space within.

And how do we find this space? We welcome our humanness. This is the third key. The first key is timelessness. The second key is space, The third key is to welcome how human we really are. We are vulnerable. We are naked. Each of us have personalities. They're only personalities, just being human. As we welcome our humanness we can come further and further inside, and we find more and more space. How do we welcome our humanness? We let go of our judgments. This is a big key. We are so judgmental about ourselves, which makes us judgmental about each other, which makes us judgmental. We really don't know. So it's really good to let go of all of our judgments. Each of us are human in a unique way. Sometimes easy, sometimes difficult, it's just being a human being. As we let go of our judgments, we can come further inside. This is the space for our awakening. The inner pilgrimage is what happens as we find more and more space. We come into emptiness. Vastness. There's so much space, inside and outside. As we come into this space, our thinking gets less and less. It just fades in the distance. As we receive the emptiness, as our mind becomes less, our heart essence comes forward.

And so the key to emptiness is to receive the heart essence, which is here. It is warm, opening, beautiful, vulnerable, light, grace, home. As we come more into the emptiness, and just receive, just be, you don't want to think about it. You don't want to watch it. You want to receive it. Let the space get bigger and bigger and bigger inside. When we find this big space inside, the challenges in daily life get smaller and smaller. As we anchor our awareness in this big emptiness inside, the story of our daily life becomes not so big, not so important. Our daily story is not so much inside of us. It's just around us. It's just a story. As we anchor our awareness in this big emptiness, we find our heart essence… being, soft, giving, open, loving. As our awareness takes anchor here, our awakening grows. As our awareness takes anchor and this big softness inside has no borders, no limits.

As we take anchor, deeper inside, our awakening unfolds here. The life of eternity, we discover our awareness has no beginning, no ending, no borders. We're connected deeply inside, to each other, to everything and everyone. The keys to our awakening, the keys to our inner pilgrimage, unlock the heart. Here the journey really begins. So much giving inside, our heart pours out everywhere inside, and keeps going inside and outside, everywhere. As we come deeper into the heart, we find more keys, more doors. Our awakening grows into more light. Deep inside, there's a light that's very, very bright. And as we breathe and receive, it grows bigger, and extends everywhere, inside and outside. We surrender to this light. We give, we offer ourselves completely to the light of our own heart. It is our shelter, our food, our essence. It is who we are.

The important key to our awakening, to this inner pilgrimage, is just to receive. Be. Enjoy as much heart as we can. We have taken the time. We have found the space. We have let go of our judgments. We breathe as human beings, vulnerable and naked. And here is our heart, with doorways into another heart, and then another heart, and more heart essence. With each breath, we offer our all and everything to the great heart. With each breath, we go deeper into this big space inside, this vastness, the space of infinite heart. We come into the very heart of our awareness. Here, we slowly awaken to who we are. The pilgrimage is beautiful. We anchor ourselves in the very heart of our awareness with each breath. Here we find our center, our soul. God inside of us, and everywhere.

Our awakening is not complicated. The pilgrimage within is not complicated. The keys take us, the keys carry us, to the very heart of our awareness. We step out of daily time, into the timelessness of the moment. Here we find more space, outside and inside. As we enjoy this big space inside, our mind gets more calm, and our heart grows in our awareness. As we let go of judgments, just be as human, as human as we are, our awareness grows again, more calm. And our heart comes more forward into our awareness. we find a vastness inside, and the very essence of our heart is everywhere. It is calm, peaceful, breathing, life, light, love. Our work is to receive the great heart inside. Then we find it everywhere around us, and in the world. Our pilgrimage is to receive, to soak, in the awakening of our own heart. We come back to the very essence, the very heart of our awareness. Here is our truth, our purpose, our journey. We offer everything inside to the great heart. We receive our own heart essence, everywhere. And in our gratitude, the journey becomes more and more beautiful.

Silence and The Journey into The Heart within Our Heart

The silence washes our awareness of thought and busyness.
Peace and quiet, we let go into the heart within our heart.
Here the great silence carries us, borderless, vastness.
We are home, the seat of trust, safety, light, our soul.

Most people think silence is just an absence of noise, some moments of peace and quiet. But actually, silence is much more, much, much more. As we take the journey into the great silence, we come into the silence of our own heart. Here is the very heart of our awareness. We are home, here. In the silence of our heart, we are completely safe. There is trust, complete trust, openness, joy, and humor. Light fills our awareness. The heart inside our heart is a silence that has no borders, no beginning, no ending. It is the seat of our soul. It is a place of infinite awareness. The heart inside our heart waits for each of us. We live in a noisy world. Mentally, we try to figure out how we're going to get from here to there. We make all kinds of plans, have all kinds of feelings, have all kinds of wishes. We get complicated. The silence of the heart inside our heart has no plans, no wishes. It's just simply being. In this deep, infinite silence, we discover silence everywhere. No matter how noisy the world, there's the presence of silence. There's silence in the trees, the flowers, in every leaf and growth of nature. The silence touches us. And we touch the silence. There's silence in each of us. No matter how busy and how noisy our personalities are, there's a presence of silence. The presence of silence is in everything and everyone. As we come into the heart inside our heart, and sit, breathe, enjoy the great quiet, the great silence, a whole other world opens to each of us. It is always giving. It is always receiving. In every breath, we are held. So much love.

I have found there's only one path to the heart inside of the heart, and this is through the silence. Every day we project our awareness into the world. We have so much thought, so much feeling and busyness. We need to take back this projection and sit in the silence. Let go of our complicated story and come back to the simplicity of this moment, the quiet, peace. As we let go of our daily story, let the chapters flow, let the pages turn, it's just a story. As we practice not holding so tightly, the silence grows inside of us. We breathe. As we go deeper into the silence within, we begin seeing the story as just a story. The people in our lives are more than personalities, more than wishes and disappointments. We see the silence in each other, the presence, the divine, the light. As we don't hold our daily stories so tightly, our hands become open for something else. There is the presence of quiet, the presence of great silence. The path to the heart inside our heart is a path of letting go. We all know this. Every day we let go of our busy mental worlds, and we come and listen to this big body of quiet. We let go of so much thought, and come into this place of no thought. We breathe.

As we come into the heart, we realize that the silence is not just empty, it's not just nothing. As we come into the silence of our heart, there's this presence, a peace without words. a quiet more quiet than quiet. There is a stillness that gives. The moment we come to our heart, we want to practice receiving what is here. As a gentle river of love, a little stream of quiet, peace surfaces within us, around us. We bathe in the river of our own heart, and slowly we discover this river, everywhere, in everyone. As we let go and journey into the heart, we discover the heart inside our heart. It is vast, big, silent. No beginning, no ending, we can breathe here. We want to focus our attention. We want to concentrate, receive the most-pure heart inside our heart. This is the source of our silence. Deep inside the most-pure heart of our heart, we come home. We come to our original awareness. It's like a newborn baby, just smiling in infinite peace. We breathe and receive our original heart. It is God inside of us. So pure, so much light, and then more light, brilliant, brilliant light. This light comes forward in our awareness. It spreads everywhere. We find the planets and the stars, the whole universe inside of us. The very center of the universe is in each of our hearts. We breathe. We receive the most-pure heart deep inside. We offer everything. We let go more and more, and then we can receive what is actually present. We are letting go into the infinite within us. This is the great silence. Inside our heart is another heart. The silence carries us here. And as we let go, there's another heart inside this heart, and the silence carries us here. And as we continue to offer and let go, there's more and more heart, just heart. That's our awareness, it truly is only heart. And the silence is everywhere. We breathe. So much peace, perfect quiet, so much love. It spreads from deep inside of us, our very center. It spreads through us and out into the world. It just keeps spreading everywhere, in everything and everyone. We give thanks for the great silence carrying us into the heart inside our heart.

Every day we want to bathe in the great silence. We want to take the time and let the silence wash our awareness. So much thinking, so much doing, so much feeling, only the silence can take it and carry it all away. As we unload our mental worlds into the great silence, as we let go and the silence washes us completely, the very heart of our awareness comes forward. We find ourselves again in the heart of our lives, the light of our awareness, clarity, openness, trust, safety. The divine becomes present, inside and outside. The great silence carries us into the heart deep inside our heart. And here's our treasure. The diamonds and jewels and gold of our own awareness. We want to put our hands into the treasure in the heart inside of our heart, and feel, receive, be golden. So much light. Everything we look for in the world is already here in the heart inside our heart. Everything we yearn for, we desire, we hope for, the silence carries us to this place inside, where everything is given. We want to breathe and receive. We let go and offer everything, and then we discover what is already present, here. We let go completely, and we discover completely who we are. So much light. So much presence. So much silence. It is always here.

The Fruit of Expanded Awareness, The Gifts of Our Awakening

As we let go of our daily story, we find our expanded awareness within. Here the gifts of our awakening begin.

The gifts of our awakening begin in our expanded awareness, this big space we find inside. Every time we let go of our daily story a little bit, don't hold our thoughts and feelings so tightly, we begin to come inside. Here we find more space, a vastness. The fruit of this expanded awareness is delicious. It is simple peace. We come deeper and deeper inside and find more space. We feel who we really are. We're much more than our daily story. In this big vastness inside, we're much more than our thoughts and our feelings. Here is our well of being. In our expanded awareness, we taste the sweetness of life itself, our heart essence.

Most people spend their days and nights, their entire lives in the daily story. Endless thoughts, so many feelings, we call this constricted awareness. The true vastness of our awareness, the ocean of being, is constricted into so many thoughts, so many feelings, so much busyness. They say that the normal person has 78,000 thoughts a day. We think way too much. Our busy mind is a filter that keeps us busy from our expanded awareness, the natural space of our vast awareness. Our busy mind is the stress we carry. We spend a lifetime of energy trying to be comfortable. But we're just riding the waves, continually adjusting, balancing, managing the world, our awareness. We have forgotten the ocean. We think the source of our problems is work, family, a neighbor, or the weather. We're looking for the source of our problems everywhere but where it is—within us, the forgotten ocean of beingness, the world's distractions from the simple peace in this moment. We think, strategize, organize, study, make an extra effort. Meanwhile the source to our problems, our expanded awareness awaits us. Instead, we live in constricted awareness, thinking too much, feeling too much. The moment we remember this big space inside, there's no need to worry so much. In our inner vastness, we don't have so many desires. Everything is here. So much is present. In our well of being, our ocean of awareness, there's no reason to think so much. We just want to be, journey deeper, adventure more into awareness itself.

The source of all of our conflicts, our problems, our stress, is our constricted awareness. We live there by habit, by culture. We need to break the habit. It's beautiful to spend time in expanded being, our big self, where there is no self. We just are. Here, our awakening begins. There are so many gifts to this awakening. They say that we should be more forgiving, but when we're in constricted mind and stress, how do we forgive? There is no room for forgiving. In our big awareness inside, the ocean of our being, it's easy to forgive, it's just natural. They say we should be more loving, more giving, but when we're in constricted awareness, riding the waves, just trying to stay comfortable, it's not so easy. But in this big space inside, it's natural to be more loving, giving, caring for each other, for ourselves. The only source to all of our troubles is we have forgotten this beautiful space deep inside, of so much being, the great ocean of awareness.

When we discover our ocean of being, our awareness with no borders, no end, the perspective of our daily story changes. It's just a story. It's okay. The perspective of our personality, our feelings, thoughts, they're just feelings, thoughts. It's part of being human. It's our human clothing. But we are much more. The gift of our awakening is this much more. As we listen to the silence of our heart, our awareness comes home. We can breathe here. We are free here. We are safe. The deep heart inside our heart is our source of trust. We create life from this place. So many possibilities. In the beauty of the heart inside our heart, we awaken. No thought, just being, we see directly. We hear directly. We touch and feel life without the filter of a busy mind. Life is heart awareness. The gift of our awakening is to go further into the very heart of our awareness. We breathe. Here there's a gentleness more gentle than gentle. Our awareness keeps spreading. We find the planets and the stars within. We find a deep center in the very core of who we are, the very core of our being. We breathe and receive the center of the universe inside of us. It radiates everywhere, inside and out.

The key to becoming free of the busy mind is to receive our awakening. Our meditation is to receive the heart inside our heart, all the light, openness, beauty. We feel it in every nerve of our being.

We feel it in everything and everyone around us. The presence of this light, the gift of our awakening is to feel this love. No matter how busy and noisy the world around us, this silence is always present. We become more sensitive to the love that is here, and the people we are with, the nature, the presence of life everywhere. Our awakening is gifts and then more gifts and then more gifts. And we breathe into a bigger and bigger heart. It expands inside of us. The heart of who we are expands everywhere. In truth, our awareness is one unlimited heart. We let go and offer everything. We go into the smile of our heart. We let go, and offer everything, and go into the garden of who we are. We keep letting go, offering, and our heart becomes more alive. We are remembering our true nature, innocence, our inner child, God inside of us, the presence of eternity.

We begin tasting the fruit of our expanded awareness the moment we let go of our daily story. We don't hold it so tightly. We come inside and our awareness rests and spreads. The fruit of our expanded awareness becomes more delicious as we come into the peace that's everywhere. Receiving this peace, our busy mind gets less. Enjoying this perfect quiet, our constricted awareness begins to let go as we spread into the ocean of being, the ocean of our awareness. Here, the fruit of being alive, the fruit of life itself, everything about it, is present. As we breathe, we come into the silence of our own heart, our awakening grows. Our awareness spreads, so much light, gentleness. We breathe. We come home.

The heart of our awareness is who we are. This is our awakening. We awaken to the great heart inside, innocent, loving, full of grace.

The gifts of our awakening grow and unfold, as our awareness finds more vastness, heart, presence, inside, in each other, and everywhere. We need to break the habit of constricted awareness. It's just a habit. and breathe into the great heart, the silence of our own heart, receive, and soak. Just soak into the awareness inside, and everywhere.

Falling, Falling into
The Gifts of Emptiness

*Falling into the vast emptiness within, frees us from all our
attention in the outer world. Falling into the profound emptiness
within offers us all the spiritual realms within our heart.*

Our meditation is all about falling, falling into the gifts of
emptiness. Normally, our daily world is pulling our awareness
outside. Every day, there is so much to do, to think about, talking,
noise. The daily world pulls our awareness outside again and again.
We think this is normal. Falling, falling into the great emptiness
inside is the balance. We come back to ourselves again, to our
wholeness. I love to meditate and watch in the season of fall, the
leaves turn color and fall from the trees. Like thoughts, life's events,
they gently let go and fall, and fall, and fall, slowly landing onto
the ground of our being. This is our practice. To come inside, let
go of the big life outside, and find a bigger life inside. We celebrate
falling by letting go of our daily story. We just don't hold it so
tight. We continue falling inside, letting go of the thoughts, our
busyness. So much to do, we just let go like a leaf on a tall tree.
We enjoy the great fall into emptiness. We continue slowly, falling
deeper within. Letting go of our judgments, the entanglements, all
the challenges in the world grow further and further away as we
fall into this big space within each of us, our emptiness.

There are so many gifts to emptiness. As we continue falling and falling and falling inside, it's so beautiful just to let go. Nothing to hold on to. It's okay. Just be and let the wind of our own breath carry us. We keep falling into profound emptiness. Our self grows smaller and smaller. We keep falling and letting go until we find this place inside of no self. No thought, just being, this is the gift of emptiness. No self. Our awareness spreads inside, and keeps spreading. There are no boundaries, no borders. We keep falling into more awareness. It is here that the gift of emptiness really begins. After no self is our true self, our being. We keep falling, falling, falling. We land in the very heart of our awareness. Our awareness spreads into beautiful wings of light. We keep falling into sacred emptiness, into the very heart of who we are. We want to breathe here, feel our essence. Emptiness, infinite awareness, sacredness, gentleness, safety, we're falling into a whole universe of trust, beauty, garden. It is here that all the spiritual realms come forward.

This is the gift of emptiness. In this big space inside, our true nature, our connection, our oneness, to all the spiritual realms is here. We want to receive this oneness. Whatever form it comes in: God, light, peace, we want to receive the pure heart inside our heart. This is the gift of emptiness. As our awareness keeps spreading deeper inside, we are falling. Letting go and falling, we fall into the infinite. Here's our source—life itself. No matter how many distractions we have in the great fall, emptiness calls us. Here, there are great big arms carrying us. The arms of our own awareness. The arms of God inside of us. The arms of our own heart hold us. Our meditation is to continue to let go, and fall into the many gifts of emptiness. To breathe emptiness, so much freedom, so much being. The daily world is far away in these moments. We remember who we are: infinite, being, love. Every nerve in our body keeps falling and letting go into the emptiness of emptiness. Into the great nothing, which is everything, here, there is enough. The very heart of our awareness is so much. We fall into the heart of our heart. It is inside and it spreads everywhere. Our hearts are connected, united. It's all one heart. We are so united in the one heart. The daily world pulls us outside. It's beautiful to fall inside, into a borderless vastness, emptiness, and come home again.

There are many gifts to emptiness, but the first of the two biggest gifts is to free us of the daily world. In emptiness we are free in the world. Our worldly self is not so big, so strong, so hard. The emptiness brings us back to softness, awareness, our heart. The second big gift of emptiness is that as our worldly self gets smaller, our spiritual self gets bigger. All the realms of spirit, love, God are found in the very heart of our awareness. Without emptiness, most people manage to just think about these realms. But with emptiness, we are these realms. We are in these realms. We just want to breathe and soak and receive as much heart inside our heart as we can. May we all practice falling, falling into greater emptiness and joy. The body of who we really are, is joy's body, love's body, body of life itself. In emptiness, all the doors, all the windows, are open. Our heart becomes larger with no borders, no boundaries. We find all inside. We find all in one another. We find all everywhere. All is the gift of emptiness.

Uncovering The Language of The Silence

Underneath our noisy world, the busy mind is the great quiet. Here the silence washes our awareness. In the silence of our heart, the language of the silence unfolds. As we listen to the silence within, in the trees, ocean, the gardens of life including in one another, a beautiful language is revealed. This is the language of the great silence.

Our meditation is uncovering the language of silence. The language of the silence is being lost more and more. There's so much noise in the world, and so much noise inside of us. So many thoughts, so much busyness, this noise covers the great silence. It covers the language of the silence. Most people, when they go into silence, they expect a message, or some words, but this is not the language of the silence. The silence is a direct experience. The silence of the trees, it's strong, giving, old. The silence of the sky is big, vast. It gives and receives so much. And each cloud gives perfect silence, presence. The silence of the ocean is also so much, so giving, it's so large. It holds our entire being, and expands us to who we really are. The silence of the mountains, includes power and strength, being and wholeness. It brings us to the mountain inside of us. And then there is the silence in each other. Each of us is a unique presence of silence. When we're not so busy thinking and judging, being our personalities, we can sit in the silence with one another. It's beautiful, very special. Inside the silence in each other are the stars and the planets, a unique presence of light. It is a real gift to receive the silence in each other.

And so how do we uncover the silence, the language of the silence? We need to slow down. We're so busy, and the silence is very still. So the first step is to really slow down. And as we slow down, the silence begins washing our awareness. All the anxiety, all the busyness, the silence invites us into a deep well of quiet. Inside this well of quiet, it continues to wash our awareness. There is clarity, being, simplicity, openness, gentleness. As we come deeper into our own silence, we begin feeling the presence of the silence everywhere, in everything, and everyone. This is where the journey really begins. This is where the language of silence begins to unfold. We discover this great vastness inside of us, the stillness, peace. We begin to experience it all around us, every day in everything and everyone. The language of the silence is always speaking in this pure quiet. Most important, we take the step into the silence of our own heart. Here is purity, safety, unending trust, God, in so many forms, all forms. This is the language of silence, the language of our own heart. It's the language of all the light inside. Love. As we come deeper into the silence of our heart, we begin seeing the heart everywhere. The silence is speaking. The presence of silence, peace, quiet, vastness. As we come into the silence of our heart, we discover a profound emptiness. No more mental worlds, no more thoughts, the filter of our personality is gone. In the profound emptiness, the silence of our heart speaks.

The language of the silence is a direct experience. With the heart of each tree, the heart of the flowers, the heart of the ocean, the heart of everything and everyone, silence is speaking. As we go deeper into the emptiness, the silence of our own heart, silence speaking without words, grows more clear. No words, no thoughts, silence speaking is a direct experience. The quiet holds us, opens us in a language of its own. The purity is pouring the water of silence over us completely. We are so clean and so innocent, we hold life in our hands, at our feet, in all of our nerves. The language of the silence is full of light. We just drink and receive this light in our whole being. We are remembering who we are.

The mystics in all traditions, they came to the silence. They came to this light, to this joy. They would just sit in the silence, and the language of the silence would hold them like a blanket of light. And inside this blanket of light, they found the treasure. The language of the silence is full of treasure, jewels, diamonds, gold. It is the treasure of life itself. The silence holds this for us. It saves us for us, it protects our treasure. As we uncover the language of the silence, the treasure is here. We find it in each other. Each of us is a treasure of silence, golden, timeless, being. Jewels. So much preciousness, our work is to come deeper and deeper into our own heart, into the perfect quiet. And then the heart of everything and everyone becomes more and more present. And the language of the silence, it speaks freely with no words. Endless beauty, deep love, God in so many forms, the silence is ever giving. We want to soak in the silence, be a sponge in the silence, just receive as much as we can of the very heart of who we are. This is all in this great, great silence.

There is a secret to uncovering the language of the silence. When we sit with a tree, it is not talking to us, it is listening. So as we listen to the silence in the tree, the silence inside of us, we come into the world of the tree, which is whole, giving, being. When we listen to the silence of the sky, it is not talking, it is listening. When we listen with the sky, it takes us into this big vastness of quiet, clarity, light. We listen to the mountains or the sea, to each other. The silence is not talking. The silence is always listening. And when we come into the listening of each other, then we experience the language, the silence in each other. It's different, very precious, unique. The silence in each other is always listening. There's so much light. So much love and God. As we listen to the heart, the silence of the heart, we discover the very heart of the silence. And here the language of the silence is present. In our world we have lots of problems with climate change, and so many things changing, and losing so many wonders in nature. We also have climate change in our own heart, and this is the loss of silence. If we lose the silence of our heart, we lose our connection to our very soul, to our being, and our connection to each other. May each of us uncover the language of the silence as a journey of goldenness. So much is being given, so much wholeness, so much treasure.

The Path of Unknowing

The pure quiet within is our source of security, safety, trust. This is the path of unknowing, finding our own wisdom in our heart. Instead of trying to know, manage, organize so much in our daily life, we have the invitation to receive the path of unknowing, the silence, emptiness, beingness inside.

Meditation is a path of the unknowing that is found in the silence of the heart. In daily life we are so busy trying to know what's going on. We spend so much energy organizing, managing, trying to control everything, trying to really know what to do next, what to do now.

There is another path. It's called the path of unknowing. And it's found in the silence of our heart. As we come inside into the pure quiet, we let go of all the needs to know what's going on, we embrace unknowing. As we let go and come into the stillness inside, more space opens up. We let go of our thoughts, our busyness. As we come into the silence of our own heart, there is a place of emptiness, of unknowing. This emptiness is very beautiful. It's very big inside, very pure, quiet. In our unknowing, we find something that is more than knowing. It is a presence. It is safety, security. As we come deeper into the silence of our heart, we come further on the path of unknowing. We can just trust here. We breathe. We feel the presence of a big heart. It starts deep inside and gets bigger and spreads as we stand in the silence of our heart, of our unknowing. We are very well here. Healing takes place. Any emotional or physical problems, we just receive the heart inside our heart. In this place of unknowing, we soak. We receive, more and more, the silence in our own heart. Normally we look outside ourselves to know, to heal, to be better, when so much is waiting inside, in this great space of silence.

We keep coming deeper in the heart of our heart. The quiet is more and more pure, beautiful. As you look deep into the path of unknowing, there's light. A special light. As we go into this light it gets bigger and brighter. Soon it is everywhere. At the very heart of the path of unknowing, is this great light. We breathe. This light washes our awareness. This light is our true awareness. This light is who we are. In the path of unknowing, we let go of all of our mental worlds, all of our worries. We let go of everything, and come more into the heart inside our heart, which is more and more light, love. This heart is so big. It continues to expand. It has no beginning, no ending, no borders. Our awareness is finding its true nature. We let go of knowing into this beautiful path of unknowing, and our awareness is the knowledge itself, our own wisdom, and knowing greater than knowing. We just stand in the heart of our own heart. Our awareness is free here. We let go and be more, unknowing. Here is our anchor, our source, our home. We trust. We are so much. The path of unknowing, the silence of our heart brings us deeper into a security, a safety, a love, that is beyond words, beyond knowing. We rest here. We are completely held in the heart of our own heart, which is God everywhere.

It is a big gift, the path of unknowing. The journey is in the silence of our own heart. We spend so much energy trying to know what's happening, trying to organize and manage and worry about this and that. The path of unknowing is a gift of freedom. We've come into the silence of our heart, and every day we went to receive the beautiful quiet. This quiet is emptiness. The path of unknowing is a path of emptiness, more space, more room. The heart of our heart comes forward in our awareness. The path of unknowing is living in the very heart of our awareness. Here we know what we know, we have the wisdom of who we are. We have the wisdom of the universe. So much is inside the heart of our heart.

The Journey of Discovering Our True Purpose

In our daily life with all our busyness we can lose our sense of purpose. The journey of discovering our purpose is in the silence of our heart. Here is the vastness, stillness, peace, and love which answers our questions and fills us with purpose.

We are on a journey to discover, what is our destiny? Why are we here? Many of us go through day by day with all the challenges doing the best we can. And we keep asking, what is my purpose? What's my destiny? Why am I here? The answer is found in the silence of our own heart. The garden that we want to find in the world begins in the garden of our heart. The light that we want to give to the world begins with the light we find inside. All the peace that we wish for, all the peace that we want, we find it in the silence of our own heart. Here, all of our questions are answered. Our journey comes home. We feel complete. In the silence of our heart, all of our thinking, all of our busyness is washed away. We find clarity here. Our awareness finds its true nature. In the silence of our heart, we find a big space inside. This vastness, this big space, is the home of the peace that we want to give to the world. This big space inside is the source of the love that we seek elsewhere. The silence of our heart is a gift that keeps giving every day. We are held here. We find gentleness here. Openness, kindness, safety, trust, knowing, we venture as deep as we can into the silence of our own heart. The daily world is washed away. We find more space, more clarity. There are worlds of love here. We receive this silence, the quiet. Inside this quiet is another quiet. It unfolds deep within. It is everywhere. This quiet is our true body, our true self is our awareness, free and infinite quiet.

Here, we feel our purpose. Each of us is a body of purpose, just being who we are. Every moment, every day, as we come deeper into the silence inside, the heart within our heart becomes more present. All of our mental worlds drift away. We let go of our mental worlds and be in this big heart inside our heart. It is full of purpose. It is our destiny. All of our questions and challenges about our daily life, they're no longer present. We just are. Each of us is a body of presence, quiet. Inside this quiet is a peace beyond words. We feel it through our whole being. It spreads everywhere. Our purpose is to be this peace, to be our awareness. Every relationship, every day, every moment, each of us gives so much by being who we are, so much heart presence, so much truth. We keep coming further within, letting go, letting go of everything and all things. We offer everything. We feel the body of our true self, our no self. Just being quiet, love, our light, we want to receive the most tender place inside. We want to be in the pure heart, inside the pure heart, which is the most-pure heart. Here is our purpose. The very heart of our awareness. The heart of our awareness is the gift we give to the world, and to ourselves.

In our daily life, with all of our busyness, everything we are thinking about and doing, we lose our sense of purpose. We wonder, what is our destiny? What life is all about? The moment we stop, and go into the silence of our heart, there's a big space. All of our thoughts, all of our busyness drifts away. And in the silence of our heart, the very presence of our heart comes more and more forward. The very heart of our awareness is here. The heart of our awareness is full of purpose. All of our questions either go away or are answered. So much quiet. Peace. Our very being, our very essence, is purpose itself. Each of us is an anchor of purpose in the world, in every conversation, every relationship and all that we do. The silence of our heart is a gift that keeps giving, as we come deeper into the great, great heart inside our heart. Here, the garden is so beautiful, giving so much. Our purpose is to be this garden in the world. May we be surrounded and may this beautiful garden grow inside and outside. May our purpose be a beautiful, beautiful light for all of us.

The Source of Our Rainbow Body, Our Awakening

In the pure silence of our heart, our Divine nature, our Rainbow Body, awakening waits for us. The journey begins clearing a great space within, emptiness. The journey continues as we receive the heart within our heart.

Meditation is the source of our rainbow body, our awakening. Many people think they have to leave their bodies to go someplace, or have to live on a tall mountain. Some think they have to give everything up or meditate six hours a day. The source of our rainbow body, our awakening, is deep in the silence of our own heart. Here there's a divine presence. It comes in many forms, many shapes. But when we experience this rainbow body, the very heart of our awareness, it's more real than real. It stays with us forever. We have dreams and great experiences in this life, but after a few weeks or months or years we forget them. But when we experience our rainbow body, our divine self, our awakening, it stays with us. It is us. It is rebuilding our true body, our true awareness. These memories, these experiences, the divine, is the structure of who we are. And it all waits for us in the silence of our heart.

There are two steps to finding the great silence inside. The first step is clearing this space. We need to practice letting go, not holding so tightly our dramas, challenges, even our joys. To find more and more room inside our hearts, we let go. Buddhists call this emptiness. The invitation is for emptiness to become our king. Let emptiness rule inside. Everything ultimately is empty of this world. All of our busyness, challenges, desires, ultimately everything is empty. As we understand this, and emptiness becomes our king, we find a great space inside. Devotees of Saint Francis call this Lady Poverty. It's not about being poor in the world, it's about feeling Lady Poverty inside, inviting us to be empty, free. In this big space inside, Lady Poverty is with us, we are not alone. She is gentle, caring, loving. It is not about suffering. It is not about being miserable, It's about joy. Lady Poverty, emptiness. It's all the same journey, finding more space inside. Every day we want to breathe into this great space inside. It has no beginning, no ending. Our awareness keeps letting go and letting go, until it finds itself going forever within.

In the great space inside, we can begin the second step. This is receiving the heart inside our heart. Many people just practice meditating, which is the first step, finding space inside. That is not enough. You could just sit in this space and watch the thoughts come and go, just keep watching and watching, and not find the great heart inside our heart. We do not find the rainbow body, our awakening. In the big space we find inside, each breath, we want to receive more of the very heart inside our heart, the heart of our awareness. Inside our heart is another heart that's pure. Here is peace. And inside this peace is another peace. Here is a stillness. And in this stillness is our rainbow body, the brilliant colors, God, so clear, so present, so much light. We keep going deeper inside, receiving more in the very heart of our heart. We keep letting go. Our awareness keeps expanding. When we can really breathe in the heart inside our heart, everything is present. So much light, love. We offer everything. We keep letting go and offering everything, allowing our awareness to get softer and softer. And we find kindness greater than any kindness, a sweetness sweeter than any sweetness. We breathe.

The very heart of our awareness is who we are. Nothing to carry, nothing to do, nothing to think about here. We just are. This is our practice. We clear the great space inside, beneath, around, above, within our busyness. We enjoy more room, more space, and vastness. We practice receiving, receiving as much of the light inside our light, in all the nerves of our body, all the nerves of our being. As we receive the great heart inside the rainbow body, our awakening, the light is inside, the light is everywhere. It's in the trees and nature, in all of us. It's in everything and everyone. We come to the very heart of this life, with no beginning and no ending. We come home again. We come home again. We want to practice receiving, being home again, no longer pulled away from who we are. Just let go and enjoy. Our heart is the floor, the ceiling, the walls, the nature, the everything in everyone.

Our rainbow body, our awakening, waits for us in the silence of our heart. So beautiful, every day our practice is to make a big space inside. We let go, we offer. There's no reason to carry so much in our awareness. We worship emptiness. We receive Lady Poverty. We breathe in a big vastness. For most of us it's easier to let go than it is to receive, but the journey is both. We let go into this big beautiful vastness inside, and here we begin to listen, receive, and take the pilgrimage in the heart inside our heart. Here there is a love greater than any love. Inside this love is a light, so brilliant, so bright. We breathe and do the best we can just to be all this light. And this light spreads. And inside this light is a kindness more kind than kind. It is a sweetness, gentleness, a peace beyond words. This piece is everywhere. We keep traveling the beautiful journey into the heart inside our heart to the very heart of our awareness. Each breath we discover more of who we are. Each of us are an anchor of this heart in the world. This is our purpose. This is our journey. May you be your rainbow body, your beautiful awakening. May you enjoy all the great silence of your heart.

Finding The Great Light

In the deep silence of our heart is a very bright light. It is through the soft eyes of our heart that we can open to this light, incredibly giving love and much more.

There is a great light found in the silence of our heart. We've all had moments of this light. Those of us who have had an NDE, near-death experience, when the mind is turned off, the light is totally here. It's just completely present. Some of us have seen or been in this light when we're with a great teacher, in a special dream, a sacred place, a deep prayer or meditation. At some times in our lives, when we are totally naked, the mind is turned off. In these moments this light is completely present. This great light is in all of us. It is found in the silence of our heart. The light is so bright, so brilliant, that our normal eyes cannot look into it. It's too bright. It's too brilliant. We must open the eyes of our soft heart. When we open the eyes of our soft heart, this light automatically comes forward. It's in all of us, each of us. It is a giving light. It gives and gives and gives like no normal light that we know about. It gives so much love that our personality cannot receive it. It's just too much. This is why we open our soft heart. Here this great light is present. Giving and giving more. In this light there is no time. The moment we walk into this light and the soft eyes of our heart, you don't know if you've been there for moments, minutes, hours, days. There's no time. It's just endless, endless light. And in this light, in the soft heart inside of us, there's no body. Our daily worldly story is just a story. It's not good or bad, better or worse. It's just a story. There's totally no judgment. When we enter the light, the great light in our heart, it washes us of all judgment, all heaviness, all thought, all these things that we carry. It's just a giving light.

It's important we take time for the great light inside each of us. In the silence of our heart, just a brief moment of this light, frees us of everything and everyone. We come back to our true nature, our true essence. We are the soft eyes of our heart. We let it go as we listen deeply into the silence inside. As we come deeper into the silence of our heart, we discover another heart. Here are the eyes of our heart. As we continue to let go and offer everything, all of our thoughts, all of our busyness, as we let it all go, the heart inside our heart takes us inside on a journey with no beginning, no ending. Just more, more heart. We breathe deep inside, becoming this light. At first it may just be a little pin drop, really small in the distance. But as we continue to offer and let go of everything, our awareness spreads bigger inside. This little pin drop begins to grow. The secret to the soft eyes of our heart is to receive this light. It is complete forgiveness, beauty, kindness, gentleness. As we receive this from the heart inside our heart, our eyes begin to open further. The heart inside our heart is giving and giving more. There is so much presence. Here all the divine qualities, all the realms are present. As we open the heart inside our heart, and let the silence hold us, carry us, we begin to remember who we really are. We discover our essence. Our daily story is just a story. There's no good, no bad. It just is what it is. But this great light inside, it waits for us. It stands inside of us and around us.

Inside this light are colors that we don't normally see with our normal eyes. You can only see these colors with the eyes of the heart. Inside this great light are angels and divine beings that we cannot see with our normal eyes. We see them with the soft, soft eyes of our heart. They're completely present. Protecting us. Our journey is to remember this great light. All these divine qualities wait for us in the silence inside. There's no beginning, no ending. It's beautiful to let go and just be in the perfect stillness. The pure quiet of the heart. As we put our feet into this pure quiet, our entire earthly being is washed and cleansed, freed. Our meditation is to free us. Here we see through the heart, we can hear through the heart, touch and smell through the heart. The world of eternity opens for each of us. We bathe, shower, walk, sit, enjoy this great light in the silence within.

We find the soft eyes of our heart opening. We see our daily world, that there's much more that is present. What we do, what we think about, all the things that keep us busy, are just a small part of our awareness. We begin to see a greater part of each of us. This light is so bright in all of us, so giving, so unique. The light is totally unique in each person in our lives. The quality of the light, the love, the presence, we enjoy special qualities, the light in everyone and everything. It's here, so present, so big. May the great light unfold inside all of us and surround us and spread everywhere.

The Three Temples

*St. Francis, mystics, contemplatives of all traditions
have discovered three temples in the silence of the heart.
There are many chapels along the way, but these three
temples are entered, received, and enjoyed by many
in the pilgrimage into the great stillness within.*

This meditation is on pure mind, pure heart. It's not as complicated as we think. Saint Francis, the mystics, and contemplatives of all traditions, they've found there are three temples in the silence of the heart. And as we come into these three temples of the silence of the heart, slowly we have pure mind and pure heart. Before entering the first temple, we take off our shoes, which is to leave our daily story outside of meditation the best we can. We leave the daily world outside as we come inside.

In the first temple of the silence of the heart, we slowly step into the great quiet. Stillness. In the first temple we sit with our daily story, all of our thoughts and feelings. The drama, the challenges, the joy pass through our mind. There's silence everywhere. And we just let our daily story be present. The quiet frees us in the story. The stillness softens all of our thoughts, all of our feelings. In the first temple, the great silence, slowly our thoughts and feelings are not so strong. They begin to fade away. And we just be present, in the beautiful quiet. We begin to see our daily story is just a story. In the stillness, our thoughts are not so heavy, our feelings are just feelings. As we come deeper into the first temple, the great quiet is here. It is the quiet of our own hearts. We just sit with our story, our thoughts and feelings, and they get smaller and smaller as the quiet gets bigger and bigger. Slowly we have a new view, a new perspective. We're not so attached to the thoughts and feelings. We're more free in the silence. We don't hold on to the story so strongly. We let it go. We let it be into the great quiet. Slowly we are preparing for the second temple.

In the second temple of the silence of the heart, here there's only vastness, space. No thoughts, no feelings are present as we come deeper into the quiet, into the perfect stillness. There is only awareness. We breathe. The second temple is no story, no thoughts, no feelings, no self, just to be, here, in the great silence. We come more into our hearts. The second temple opens us to our true nature. Just awareness, no beginning, no ending, no time is present. Our awareness has no top, no bottom, no sides. It is vast, everywhere. The second temple of the heart frees us. We're remembering our true essence, just awareness. We just are. As we sit in the perfect stillness, it washes our awareness. We are more open, free, available to our true heart. The second temple is wonderful. There's so much peace here. Nothing to think about, nothing to do. We are. The second temple is the temple of transition. It prepares us for the third temple. In the second temple we can do our work. We can let go. We can offer. We feel our awareness and receive more of our heart. Slowly, slowly, as we have no mind, just awareness, no story, just being. The true heart inside our heart comes forward. This is the third temple.

The third temple is the actual presence of God inside of us. It's not something we can do or make happen. We can just be in the first temple, the second temple, and then the third temple opens on its own, on its own accord. It's something beyond us. It is in us and yet beyond us. The third temple is a part of us but is something much greater than us. In the third temple is just God. In many forms, Saint Francis, mystics of all traditions in their little cave on the mountaintop or in the woods, discovered the third temple. The contemplatives of all kinds know the third temple. Here, our awareness just is. We are including a great light deep inside of us. A presence of love, a very pure stillness, a very wonderful peace is inside and all around us. In the third temple, God inside of us, God in nature, God in all, radiates from within outward in the great silence.

In the silence of the heart, there are three temples. Saint Francis, the mystics, the contemplatives, and all traditions, they know these temples. Along the way there are many chapels. Each of us finds special chapels, sacred places, teachers, chapels of all kinds. But there are three distinct temples on the path into the heart inside our heart. The first temple, we enter the silence with our daily story, all of our thoughts and feelings, and we sit in the great quiet. And slowly, slowly, the story is not so strong. The thoughts and feelings are not so heavy. Slowly, slowly, the stillness frees us of so much story, so much thought and feeling. We sit in the first temple and the quiet holds us deeply. And our mental busyness gets less and less and less. And slowly we come into the second temple of the silence of our heart. In this temple there is only awareness. We find more and more space, more and more quiet. The stillness has freed us of our story. There's a vastness of just being. So much peace. The second temple is a transition temple from this round to the realm of eternity. The second temple is beautiful, wonderful. Here, slowly, we become free of this body as we enter another body, which is the third temple. The third temple is the actual presence of God. It is our golden body, our light body, our Christ body. There are no names for it really, it has no name, it is just so much God.

We have to take our time going through these temples, there's no hurry. You can spend hours, days, weeks, months in the first temple, there's no hurry. In the second temple, there's no hurry. And the third temple you never know when it begins, where it begins, and where it brings us.

It's very interesting; the basilica of Saint Francis, where Saint Francis is buried, in the first church, in the upper church, is the story of Saint Francis painted on all the walls. It is the first temple. Then as you go downstairs, deeper inside into the second church, there is all the altars, Mary, you know, offerings, candles, masses, everything is taking place in the second church. The story is becoming free to just presence, to just peace, to just God. And then you go downstairs once more into the tomb of Saint Francis. It is just peace. It is the third church.

Millions, literally millions, of pilgrims come every year for many, many hundreds of years. They start in the first church, they go into the second church, and slowly they enter the tomb of Saint Francis. And here there's an incredible presence, there's so much peace. It's just pure presence. This is tradition as in Hindu temples, Buddhist ashrams and temples, we find it in Bali. It is the path for each of us. To walk gently into the great silence of our hearts. Into the three jewels, the first temple, the second temple, and finally the third temple.

The Steps into The Temple of Our Heart

---

*Leaving our daily world at the door, we step into a
vastness, pure stillness in the temple of our heart.
Here our awareness discovers its true nature,
peaceful, endless beingness, and much more.*

We're in Assisi, Italy, the home of Saint Francis and Saint Claire.
We're surrounded by ancient Roman ruins. There's so much peace
here. So much pure quiet. Saint Francis used to meditate on the
hill above Assisi, and on hilltops all over central Italy. On [Italian
mountain names], on hilltops all over Italy he'd go into a little cave
and sit in the great quiet. Today's meditation is on the steps into
the temple of our own heart, into the great quiet inside. The steps
approaching the temple of our heart are as important as the steps
we take once inside. You want to go into the temple of our heart
with empty hands and naked feet. You don't want to carry anything
into the temple. You want to let go of all that we're carrying, all that
we're working with, and you want to go in with naked feet, which
means you want to leave the daily world behind and approach the
temple at simplicity, nakedness, just being ourselves. The steps
before we enter the temple determine what we find inside the
temple. We want to let go of our daily story. Just leave it outside
the best we can. It's just a story, page by page, chapter by chapter,

always changing. We leave it outside the temple of our heart. We offer everything. We empty all the pockets, all the shells, all the closets inside the best we can. And slowly, we step into the great quiet in the temple of our own heart.

As we enter the door, the great quiet washes our awareness. The moment we enter the door of the golden temple of our heart, the silence is so pure. It just wipes everything away but the silence itself. Our awareness lets go as slowly we come deeper, deeper into the quiet of our own heart. There's a stillness here. It's so pure. Quiet. As we listen deeply into the stillness, our awareness gets softer, more open, more gentle. We keep letting go more and more and more of everything but awareness itself. The great silence inside. It spreads our awareness, opens us, as we find more and more space inside, vastness. We go deeper and deeper into the quiet which is more than quiet. As we come into the heart of our temple and to the temple of our heart, our awareness keeps spreading and spreading in all directions. No beginning, no ending. There's so much presence, so much quiet. There's no time here. No beginning, no ending, no top, no bottom. We just breathe our own awareness, which is all, which is connected to everyone and everything. In the temple of our heart, we are free.

We breathe. We keep coming deeper and deeper inside, and in the distance we see a bright light, a very bright light, and it keeps growing, and it's coming closer to us, or are we going closer to it? The light is very, very bright. This is the light of our true awareness, the light of our own temple of the heart inside our heart. We breathe and we see the light from deep inside. It is so bright. So much as we offer everything, offer all who we are, we

89

let go and offer everything, we come more and more into our inner temple. Here there's so much God. Love, peace, whatever we want to call it. We are held here. In the great silence of the temple of our heart. We're coming more and more into our own home. Safe and true. The journey really begins here. Remembering our true nature. Feeling our essence. Just being in the pure quiet inside the quiet.

As we step into the temple of silence in our hearts, the great silence washes us so completely. The pure quiet untangles the knots. The light and the stillness, it is food for our nerves, for our being. We want to be very patient with our meditation. Don't judge it, don't analyze it, just be in the temple of our own hearts. Here we discover our own goldenness. Vastness. Just simple peace. Slowly, slowly, this simple peace becomes our anchor. Instead of our mind taking off in all these realms of thought and feeling, our awareness becomes more and more anchored in the temple of our own heart and simple peace. This peace we bring wherever we are and to every conversation, every relationship. Each of us are anchors of peace in this world.

Uncovering The Great
Light Within

*As we don't hold so strongly our daily story, as we let
go of our mental worlds, we discover another world
within our hearts. Here a vastness, peace, and deep
silence uncovers the great light within. This light is
brilliant, full of love, and presence beyond words.*

We are uncovering the great light that is inside each of us. We've all had moments in this great light. It could be in meditation or a prayer. People who had a near-death experience, when the mind is just turned off, suddenly the awareness finds incredible light. But we don't need a near-death experience. This light is deep in the heart of each of us. The question is how to uncover the light. The very essence of our awareness is light. Clarity. Peace. Our meditation practice is not holding so tightly our daily story. Let the pages turn, the chapters turn, let the daily story move. We let go and offer all of our busyness. We let go and offer thoughts, fears, judgments, all these things that keep our mind busy. And slowly we come more inside, into this moment. We breathe deeply into our own hearts. This is the source of the light.

As we offer all of our mental worlds, our awareness comes deeper inside. We find more space. Just being present, we can be in the heart inside our heart. Here is a very fine point of light. Slowly it grows and grows bigger and bigger. It's not clear whether we're going into the light or the light is coming into us. It doesn't matter. We just receive as much light as we can. And what is this light? It is a great silence. A stillness that is inside stillness. This light is peace. It is the pure quiet inside of peace. As we go deeper light gets bigger and brighter. It is so bright we can't look into it. This is the very heart of our awareness. It's uncovered as we just practice receiving the peace and quiet, stillness, and look as deeply into the light as we can. We breathe. Our awareness is so big inside, so vast. The light opens more light. We soak in this light. We are this light. It is our true body. Our essence. Our awareness when we're free. It is all. It is all in us. It's everywhere. You let go into the light. We let go of everything into the light.

It's difficult to find words for this light. In this light there's no self for the words to come. But it is the peace that is inside of peace. It is the stillness that's inside of silence. Clarity, purity, a love that is more gentle or giving than our personality is used to. Love is so present, so whole. There's a secret to uncovering this love, uncovering this great light. Whatever we find inside in the heart inside our heart, you offer it in our meditation. We offer it in our prayer. It begins to grow inside. We offer this light in our words, relationships, the conversations in daily life. This light gets slowly brighter and bigger.

In the beginning the light is just like a couple flowers. But it's giving flowers. Slowly the light becomes like a garden, so giving, so big. As we continue to offer the light, in our meditation, offer it all. The garden becomes a valley of light. It washes us, frees us. So much light, the valley garden becomes a valley of light, then a world of light. Slowly, we are a life of light. We keep offering it and it grows stronger and bigger inside. So instead of grabbing on to the light, wanting the light, the secret to uncovering it is to offer it. Everything we find in the heart inside our heart, we offer it and it grows bigger, very beautiful.

Monastery without Walls

We are called to make a life honoring and sheltering our hearts, to make our daily life a monastery, a monastery without walls.

All of us, we need to have our own monastery in our lives. We need to look at our lives and see if we give shelter to our hearts. Do we give shelter to our souls? Do we have time for the lightness of our being, to be fully aware of how present, how much peace is here right now in this moment? We look at our lives in terms of how much income we have, or what we're doing and everybody else is doing. I invite us to look at our lives as a monastery. A monastery without walls, but nevertheless a monastery, where our hearts can fully feel who we are in the life around us. And more important where our souls feel sheltered, protected, honored. Where we can listen deeply. And slowly, slowly, no matter what our daily life is like, hopefully it becomes a life more and more just for the soul. The opportunity is to feel how much and how great the presence of silence is right now.

Every time we go into meditation, we're actually walking into the monastery inside. As we let go of the noise of the world, there's a great silence. This silence is our real monastery, our inner monastery. Our meditation is the shelter for our soul. It's not important how much we do or we think, or if something special to happen. You just want to sit, and be, in your own inner monastery. As we feel the silence in us and around us, slowly we feel more of the peace that is here, that is present. This peace dissolves the noise. The noise within us and in the world fades into the background as we go more into the silence of our own heart. Our heart is the inner walls to our monastery. No matter how old we are, or young we are, actually our heart, our soul, is very old. It's lifetimes. It has no beginning, no ending. So as we slowly sit in the silence of our heart, here there is no time. Our monastery is ancient, and at the same time it is new. There's a special quiet to the monastery. A special presence. There's the light, our angels, the high beings that may be with us. Every day we want to spend time, take the opportunity, to be in the shelter of our own monastery, in the presence of our own soul.

As we come deeper into who we are, the doors and windows and landscape of our soul becomes more present. Every day it's a little different. The gentleness is so beautiful. The quiet is full of light, purity. It washes everything in the monastery, all the walls, all the noise outside the monastery, the purity of the quiet inside. There's so much light. Just to be in the presence of our own soul, it emanates love. Forgiveness for every part of us, for every part of our monastery, forgiveness for every part of our daily life. Our soul emanates this love, this forgiveness. In the very middle of our monastery, in the very essence of our soul, there's a stillness. And inside the stillness is another stillness. There are no words here. It just feels so safe, so whole. To sit inside our own monastery, in the shelter of the silence, and just be. We feel the landscape, the body of our own soul. Somehow the body of our own soul is the body of everyone and everything. There's no separation, it's just connection. The stillness weaves us with everyone and everything, in perfect quiet. Light, stillness, no matter where we are, we're all living in the same monastery without walls. In the shelter of the silence, just being here in this moment, breathing, the sacredness of our souls holds us and protects us. Our awareness is free. We just breathe and enjoy the sacredness of our own monastery. The meditation, this moment, it is giving. It is giving so much. We just want to be in this moment.

We are invited to look at our life as if it is a holy monastery. Do we give shelter to our souls? Do we honor and protect the life of our soul? In a monastery, there are things to do. The monks and nuns, the people are busy. But it's organized around the life of the soul. Many times during the day, the bells ring. And when the bells ring, you're reminded of this moment. The soul is breathing. And then there are times during the day for meditation and prayer. Life is organized around the soul. We, too, deserve a life of the soul. Our monastic walls are every moment we find silence during the day. Finding silence is our monastic wall. You can be at the table, in a park, in meditation, silence is the walls of our monastery. Our monastery has no walls but pure silence. And in the sacredness of the silence, in the moment of now, we come to our original light. We breathe. So much innocence, the walls fall down that separates us from our soul. Only the monastery is left. This is the power of silence, the beauty of peace. The quiet holds us deeply.

In our monastery we can listen. The moment we listen, we receive so much sacredness. Infinite love, being, whether we know it or not, each of us, we all live in a monastery. The life of our soul, it's beautiful to recognize it, to appreciate, have gratitude, and most important, to receive the shelter that we're given for our own soul.

The Path to An
Uncomplicated Life

*The journey to an uncomplicated life begins by living
in this moment. Here much of the worries and desires
we carry begin to fall away. As we recognize the beauty,
silence, simple peace that is present, our awareness
becomes lighter, clearer, more trusting. Our meditation
is to receive the pure heart within our heart. This is our
path, our source of being, free, living in the heart of life.*

Today's meditation is finding freedom from a complicated life. We all get so complicated. It has become more and more clear, the path to being free from a complicated life, begins by living more in the moment. This is a practice to live in this moment. As we breathe and live in the moment, a lot of the baggage we carry begins to drop off. Just being here in this moment, a lot of the little things that keep us busy begin drifting away. We just breathe and be here, now. Normally we run away in conversation, in thoughts, or all the things we want to do or shouldn't do. This moment brings the conversation back to here. There really is no conversation, more than being here now. There's so much in this moment, just to be.

Being present begins to free us from lots of things we can let go of. As we be here in this moment, it's special to recognize the beauty of the moment. Just to be in the moment and see the beauty that is here. Around us, the beauty inside, beauty is the presence of God. As we drink beauty, it washes our awareness. Our complicated self gets less and less. As we enjoy the beauty in this moment, there's so much presence of beauty, of life, of God. And as we go into the beauty of this moment, we find stillness. We just want to be still and receive the beauty in this moment. In stillness our complicated life dissolves. It fades in the distance. In the pure quiet of stillness, the beauty becomes more evident. The moment becomes more moments, more now. We are called to go further into the stillness within. As we really breathe in the stillness, there's more space inside that is perfectly still, quiet. The silence washes a lot inside. The silence makes space. The moment is full of silence, always. No matter how noisy the world, the silence vacuums up all the stuff inside. The silence wipes away all the complicated being inside. The stillness has a special quality. Light, freedom, vastness, slowly we get to the source of an uncomplicated life.

The source that finally really frees us is the heart inside our heart. The moment opens the door to this. Our beautiful, still, deep heart inside our heart. The key to freeing ourselves of a complicated life is receiving the heart inside our heart. The pure heart inside dissolves all the knots. History goes away. Everything we carry is dissolved in the pure heart inside our heart. We don't need to worry about it. We don't need to figure it out. We don't need to talk about it. We don't even need to understand it. Our practice is to receive the heart of our hearts through our whole being. Just to go deeper into our heart and breathe, we receive as much light as we can. Gentleness. Love.

Inside the heart inside our heart there's a very pure well of being. We bring it into the world with us. Completely innocent. Fresh. Light. Open. Clear. More peaceful than peace. Our meditation is practicing receiving this pure heart inside the heart. This is the path to the uncomplicated life. It brings us more into this moment. More into the beauty, more stillness, heart, there is much light here for each of us to receive. To absorb with each breath. e've found the source to all of our questions, the source that ends the struggle, the source that washes away the complicated life. It is this deep well in the heart of our heart. Here is another heart and then another heart. And then another heart that has no beginning, no ending. There's no time.

We drink this beautiful heart into every nerve, every part of ourselves, every everything, every inch of our life. And everything but the heart slowly fades away. There is only the very heart of our life.

The path to the uncomplicated life begins here, now, in this moment. The moment we are here, now, a lot begins to fall away. A lot begins just to be gone. This moment is so freeing from the past and the future. This moment is so much. This is a practice, not to run away in conversation, not to let our thoughts carry us someplace else, but just to be here. In this moment, we recognize the beauty, the sky, the nature, in each other. Beauty in all forms is the actual presence of God. This beauty only exists in the moment. So the moment is actually the door to complete God, all God, all beauty. And in this beauty, we find a special stillness, a special silence. No matter how noisy and busy the world, this silence is always present. It is the core of our awareness, the very essence of our heart. It is a stillness that is peace expressing itself. A stillness that is the body of peace. We breathe. And the very heart of our awareness is here. Our practice is to journey into the heart inside our heart, where there are no walls, no boundaries, no obstacles, only more and more heart. No borders, the freedom from all the obstacles, from all the complications, from all the drama, the pain we carry, the worries and the desires, all the stuff... is in one little small moment of pure heart. We take this pure heart and hold it as our treasure. There's a light that radiates everywhere inside and out. We wash our hands and feet in the pure heart inside of us, the pure heart in each of us, the pure heart that is everywhere. All of this builds our awareness, strengthens our awareness, clarifies our awareness. Our trust grows here. The source is the heart inside our heart. Greater than any challenge we face, so much beauty, silence, so much God.

How to Care for Our Open Heart?

How do we care for our open heart? It is through receiving the golden heart within our heart that we find the nourishment, protection, and vastness of our true being.

Today's meditation is, how do we live with an open heart? New York City is a good test for this. Yesterday we were walking down the street, and there's a lady in the corner just crying hysterically. Everybody was walking by her as if she was not there. A little bit later, we took the subway. Everybody was squished into the subway car, lots of noise, everything happening. We come upstairs out of the subway and there's a young man on a walker. And I go over to say hello to him, "How are you doing today?" He looked at me like I was from another world. Like, you don't ask this, we don't do that. My brother explained that in New York City, everybody just keeps their head down. They keep going and they don't talk to each other. There's too much going on. And then, interestingly, we go into the park across the street and it's another world. In the park, people talk to each other. We met some Italians. We met some families. People are friendly and they talk to one another. In the park there's beautiful nature, lots of gardens, flowers. And you go further in the park and there's no noise. It's really quiet. This moment was a real lesson. Nature washes the noise from our bodies, from our nerves. Nature washes our awareness. The park is a big gift in New York City.

So today's meditation is how do we take care of our open heart so that we won't become too hard or shut down to the world around us. The most important thing is to recognize the importance of our heart. To breathe and feel the presence of our heart, and the presence of heart all around us, in the city and across the street in the park. As we feel the presence of our own heart, more space begins to open up inside. This space is our interior life, it's our garden. It is the garden of who we are. If we become too closed down, the space becomes too small, and pretty soon, before we know it, our heart almost disappears. So our meditation always begins finding the vastness inside. In this vastness we begin listening to the silence of our own being. The silence spreads and we find more space inside. In the vastness, we find within is a special quality of stillness. Quiet. Here our heart can really begin to breathe again. We open, smile. This is the beginning of the treasure hunt into the heart inside our heart. Most people live separate from their hearts, just a few moments here and there, a few kind words, a little bit of joy. But we're on a grand journey. This is into the golden heart deep inside our heart. It is the golden heart that frees us from all the knots, the endless thoughts, the entanglements we have inside. It is the golden heart inside our heart that we want to breathe into. Here is our treasure room. It is a space with no beginning, no ending, no borders.

In this golden room, there is no time. Our awareness has a body of goldenness and light. The daily life, all the noise of the city is far away. We are remembering our true essence, the very heart of our awareness. We want to put our hands into the golden room, into the golden heart inside. We put our feet in the golden room and walk further and further into the beautiful peace. So much light, golden light, there is only awareness, no thoughts. Only now, only the present is in the golden room inside our heart. We are safe here. Completely safe. We come home here. We breathe and continue to let go. We breathe and let go and let go into more goldenness, more heart. This is our source. Our journey begins and ends here. Our awareness is everywhere. Inside and outside, in the park, in the city, and the walls and the apartments in the sky. It's just awareness. And it's all full of golden grace. Golden light. The silence is greater than any noise. The silence is larger than any disturbance. The silence is complete, whole. So much beauty here, we continue to let go, and just be. It's as if we are forever in the heart inside of us. This is how we take care of our heart. By making the great journey, inside our heart where everything is golden, light, peace. We feel the pure being in our whole body and all of our nerves. The golden heart is inside and outside. It holds us, protects us. It's our real skin, our real body. So much light and gentleness. There is much grace to share with each other. We take care of our open heart sitting in the grace of our golden being, God inside of us, God everywhere.

In today's world, more than ever, we ask, how do we take care of our open heart? Do we live full time in the city or spend more time in nature? Do we live alone or with others? Do we meditate? How much or how often every day? Each of us find the path best for us. Nevertheless, we are making the great journey into the heart inside our heart. In the golden room, we can take care of our awareness. In the golden room we can breathe freely. The golden light is everywhere. The room has no top, no bottom, no size. It's so vast inside. The golden heart, we feel, is spreading, deeper, taller, wider. We're completely held here. So much goldenness, so much light, this is how we take care of ourselves in this world. By making the journey into a greater world, the world of infinite heart. It is this infinite heart, we take with us on the journey after we leave these bodies, these personalities. After we leave our daily story, it's the infinite heart of who we are that we take with us. This is how we take care of ourselves.

Discovering The Path of Grace

Take the path of discovering grace and life's obstacles, worries, and challenges decrease. Our awareness of grace increases. Grace washes our awareness, bringing us to the very heart of awareness, the heart of life.

Meditation can be discovering the presence of grace. It's actually a path of learning how to be with the grace that is here. Hard to define what grace is, but it is something beyond us, something out of our control. It can be a sudden feeling of peace inside or around us. It can be the sky opening up to a beautiful sunrise, sunset, or rain. It can be an unexpected phone call, a letter, visit, or opportunity. Grace can be having breakfast with our partner. This is grace. A few days ago we were an hour or so outside of New York City with my brother in his car, enjoying the colors of fall. Suddenly the car goes dead, starts smoking. We are way out in the countryside. Just as we get out of the car on a remote road, a car pulls up and someone shouts, "Hey can we help you?" They proceeded to take us to the only repair shop in the area and then drove us back to New York. That's grace. Grace comes in big ways and small ways. There's always a path. Discovering grace, we're usually too busy. Life is too complicated. The grace may be here but it passes us by. We don't notice.

So the first step in the path of grace is the practice of being very present. As we practice being here, now, we become more aware. Grace is present with us in the present moment in a perfect stillness. Even if the world is noisy and complicated as we become present there's a great stillness. This stillness is light. This light is a magnet for grace. As we receive the light in this moment, we become aware that there is grace here. This grace is peace without borders, without end. This grace is a big space we find inside. We can let go of our daily story, all of our entanglements. As we are in this moment, in the stillness, the light, the peace, more space opens inside of us. We feel a great vastness inside. Often in a moment of emptiness, grace becomes more present. We're more present, more available. Emptiness is the best friend of grace. If we're full of things, things to do, things to think about, just things, the grace can seem very far away. But in our emptiness, we are available. Actually, we are never separate from grace. It's just our mind, our busyness, all the things that occupy our attention that maintain the illusion of separation. Emptiness heals the separation. The grace is here, present. Actually, grace is the presence of heart, our heart or whatever form heartfulness is present.

In our emptiness, our own heart comes forward in our awareness. As our heart comes forward, the very heart of our awareness is here. We see the heart all around us, in each other, in nature. We feel the presence of our heart, the heart of life. Grace unfolds. It is actually big, full of life, love. We go deeper into the heart within our heart, here's a cup of pure grace. We want to drink from this cup, feeling the grace pouring all over us, in light, peace, pure being. Our meditation is to drink from the cup of grace, waiting for us. We find this cup everywhere in life. There are many paths in life but the path of discovering grace is powerful, very special. Every time we become available and we receive grace, it washes our awareness. It purifies our awareness. It opens us to more grace. Our difficulties get smaller. Our worries go more in the distance. They fade away. The challenges are not so big. Our awareness of grace grows. It is more present, abundant, real in our lives, Grace begins by practicing being in this moment, practicing being very present. As we are present, we discover a stillness. In the stillness is lots of light, very brilliant, bright light. In this light is peace. This peace opens more space inside and outside. Life becomes less complicated. We have more simplicity. The very heart of our awareness comes more forward, more clear. The very heart of life is present. This is the source of grace. If we drink from the cup of grace every day there's more magic in our lives, wonder, simple peace. We feel connected to ourselves, to something greater. Grace is the connection. Grace connects us to life in such a great big way.

The Path to Our Inner Garden

*Our inner garden calls us. It is our ground of being.
Here our inner garden grows, simple peace and
beauty beyond words await us. Our meditation is to
be in our ground of being and receive the light of the
heart. The path to our inner garden is unfolding.*

Meditation is a path to our inner garden. For everyone, life is change. Work is changing. Health is changing. At one time or another, everything seems to be changing. There's no clear path. We have moments of our inner garden, moments of peace, of beauty, but there is no clear path to the inner garden. Slowly, slowly, however, as we find our inner garden, we find life as a garden more everywhere in our daily life.

The first step to the inner garden, the most important step, is remembering our ground of being. In meditation and every day, we want to feel our true ground inside. Just being, grounded, brings us back home. Most people, their ground is in their work, their health, their bank accounts and their homes. And all of this is changing. The daily life is changing so much, they don't feel their ground. Our garden grows in the ground. So every day when we meditate, every day in our daily life, we remember our true ground within us, of just being are important steps. It's a beautiful feeling, the soil of who we are. The daily world pulls our attention outside. Our ground of being brings us back, back inside. And as we get to know our ground of being, the most important thing is to let go of our judgments. Every garden has rocks in it. Sometimes everything grows, sometimes seemingly nothing grows. We have so many judgments about ourselves, others. We're just human beings. It's okay to have rocks in our ground of being. Rocks are normal. They're natural. So all of our judgments about what we do or what we couldn't do, our judgments about others, it's important to let it all go and just be in our ground, our ground of being. If we have a whole row of flowers growing, or one flower growing, it's not so important. When we're in our ground of being, everything is okay. We put our hands and our feet in the soil and it's rich. Our ground of being is full of possibility, full of potential, full of beauty. In this moment, as we feel our ground of being, we feel how big it is inside. It has really no borders. Our being is large. We feel the presence of our ground of being.

The garden needs light. And so the second step in our path to the big inner garden is going deep into our ground of being, and here we find our hearts. Our hearts are the source of light for the inner garden. We breathe and feel the peace inside. We go deeper into this peace. It has a quality of stillness, purity. Our being feels like velvet, feathers, soft, water. Our inner garden is very present here. And as we keep inside the heart, there is another heart, and another heart, and as we come deeper inside, there's this light. It is this light that nourishes our ground of being. It is the light of our own heart. It's full of grace. It's full of seeds, seeds of possibility. As we receive the light of our own heart, this grace, the seeds enter our ground of being. This is where the garden grows.

Receiving the light of our own heart, we keep coming further into the garden as this light grows stronger, brighter, more open. This light shines through our entire being, to our entire self. It is so bright that our thoughts fade into the distance like stars. And this is like the sun inside of us. Actually, it's brighter than the sun, our ground of being in the big heart inside of our heart. We breathe. We feel the ground everywhere inside and outside. Just being, we enjoy simply being here in this moment. We look into our heart and see and receive as much of the light as we can. It spreads everywhere, inside and outside. This is the magic of our inner garden. Here everything is present. So much quiet. It is food for our nerves. It heals our body. It softens all of our thoughts. This light is the very heart of our awareness. We go in the very center in the very heart of our awareness, and it spreads. It's vast. It's the whole universe inside of us. And as we feel our ground of being, we are the very center. We feel centered, deep in ourselves. It's beautiful to sit in our own center, the center of the universe, the source of so much light, so much being. Everything good is present here.

Every day we want to remember the path to our inner garden. Here we can let the world move and change as we come home again and again. Inside our ground of being is where the garden grows. It's very strong, clear, trusting, silent. And as we come deeper into our ground of being we feel the source of our garden, of all the beauty, of all the flowers of life. We come into the heart inside our heart. Here, there is much light. Very bright. Grace. The seeds of all possibility. New doors, new opportunities, new life begins here in the heart inside our heart. We receive the grace, the seeds. Here's our source of healing. Our source of new beginnings. The source of our source. It spreads inside of us and it spreads everywhere. As we come to our inner garden, we see it more in everyday life. It's in the simple moments, in nature, our walks, our relationships, with our partner, friends. We see the beauty of the garden present in all our life.

Learning The Language
of Eternity

---

*We know eternity is real but we have only moments
or brief experiences. We can learn the language of
eternity and enjoy the great peace, the love in our
awareness. The language of eternity begins with a deep
listening, receiving, in the heart within our heart.*

Meditation is actually a practice in the language of eternity. It is through the language that the reality of eternity takes form and takes shape. It is through the subtle language of meditation that we know reality. But most of us, we don't really know the language of eternity. We know eternity is real, that these bodies are temporary. We know someday the body of our awareness goes on without our body. We know that our daily story, page after page, chapter after chapter, will come to an end and the story of our awareness will continue. We have moments of understanding eternity. We have experiences. But we don't really know the language of eternity. It's beautiful to learn the language of eternity. It's a very different language. It requires no memorization and study. It requires our experience, our commitment to knowing deeply. It is a pilgrimage inside.

The language of eternity begins in silence. This silence is not the absence of noise. It is a special silence of the heart. As we come into the heart and go into the silence, we begin learning the language. It's not a language of speaking more, or learning. It's more of a language of listening. Receiving. As we come deeper into the silence of our heart, the listening leads us to new words, new experiences. Listening brings us into a profound emptiness. Here eternity becomes very present. As we become more present in the silence of our heart, another heart opens. In this heart is a big space. This is the space of eternity. We breathe. Our awareness in other languages is constricted, but our awareness in the language of eternity spreads bigger and bigger. It has no beginning, no ending. As we listen into the silence of our heart, the language of eternity has no time. It is a bell ringing without sound. It is a quiet that is so pure. As we learn the language of eternity, something inside of us feels, oh, it's so wonderful, so beautiful. The beauty and the love we find in the world reminds us of the language of eternity. The givingness and the support we give each other reminds us of the language of eternity. It is so giving, so holding, so complete.

As we continue listening and learning more of the language of eternity, we are taken on a journey with no beginning, no ending. It's different from moment to moment. It can be very peaceful, like you drop into a well of bottomless peace. It can be very loving, like the moments we felt the most love in this world, with our family, parents, friends, or partner. Multiply this times a hundred, so much love. The language of eternity is a continual letting go into more of our heart. It's a continual offering. With everything we find, we find more that is being offered. The language of eternity is stepping into an unknown that is completely known. It is as if it has always been, always will be. It can never be taken away.

The language of eternity is the very heart of our awareness. Here, we continue to listen. It's not a mental listening. It's our heart receiving. How available can we be? As our awareness stretches to the planets and stars of the universe, we become more and more available. We receive. The language of eternity is a completeness, a whole universe inside of us.

We continue to let go. There's light, grace, understanding, knowing, freedom. The language of eternity grows and grows inside of us, as we give ourselves completely to the heart inside our heart. As we just keep giving more of ourselves to the heart in each other, the heart in the world, the heart in life. Eternity speaks in the silence. Light, stillness, the language of eternity is like crystals, radiating. Everything is radiating. Every day we want to take a bath in this language, wash ourselves in this language. Just be completely wet in the language of eternity. Here, everything good is present. There is only yes. And as we fall into the language of eternity, we're falling into more and more yes. There is only yes. It is a huge mountain of yes. A sea of yes, a planet, a universe of yes. We are all invited into the great pilgrimage as we learn the language of eternity.

The language of eternity may seem like a foreign language. And yet we already know it. As we come deeper into the language of eternity, we realize it's always been here. It is with us. It is our original language. It is our first language. We come into the world completely immersed in the language of eternity. Slowly, slowly, the world pushes and pulls our awareness, and we separate from this place, this beautiful place, this garden in our hearts. The language of eternity brings us back to the original garden. There's so much to experience here. As we let go of our judgments, we find patience. As we let go of our expectations, we find peace. All separateness is healed in the language of eternity. Our loneliness comes from constricted thought. But the language of eternity spreads our awareness into vastness. There's no separateness. We spread into much space inside and outside. In the trees, nature, with friends and family, everything and everyone is part of the body of eternity, the body of life. The language of eternity in gratitude, opens again and again and again inside of us. In gratitude, we melt. And we breathe. We enjoy. We're all learning this language together. It's a foreign language, until we realize it's not foreign at all. It's who we are. It's our true nature, our original awareness.

Whole Heart Meditation

Whole heart meditation empties our heart of everything but the heart itself. We become the very heart of our awareness. Our judgments place large rocks in the river of our awareness. Forgiveness, gentleness, kindness moves some of these obstacles aside. Whole heart meditation clears our awareness of all that is not our pure heart. Our awareness becomes light, our true nature, innocent, giving, whole.

Meditation is the whole heart meditation. It's very special. I don't think I've ever shared this publicly before. So maybe we can all enjoy it. There are many small things that we do to keep the heart clear. For the river of our awareness to be clear, we let go of judgments. One judgment can be like a giant stone in the river of our awareness. This one stone affects the river, where it goes, all who are present. It can affect many people. We let go of our judgments the best we can about ourselves and each other. We practice forgiveness for ourselves and each other. Just a little forgiveness can move the stone in our river of awareness to the side. It can loosen up. It moves. It doesn't stay there. We are more kind and gentle, loving and giving with ourselves and each other. All of this helps clean the river of our awareness. We don't carry so much in our hearts. The whole heart meditation, empties our heart of everything but the heart itself. It's very powerful. Whether we do it for five minutes a day or twenty-five minutes or longer. It's not how long we do it. It's how we do the whole heart meditation.

Whole heart meditation is in and through all of the heart. As we breathe into our heart, all of our thoughts, everything we're carrying is being washed away in light. As we exhale in our heart, all the rocks in the river of our awareness, all the entanglements, all that is unnecessary is being washed away. We breathe deeper into the heart of our heart, more light comes. We exhale into the light of our heart. This light is much greater than any obstacle. It is the truth. It is who we are. We breathe into our heart. And we exhale in our heart. The light grows bigger. It is everywhere, inside and outside. It has no beginning, no ending, no boundaries, no borders. We breathe into our heart. We exhale in the heart. Here there is no time. A perfect stillness, quiet, we breathe in the light. We exhale in the light. So many realms of light are right here, now. The river of our awareness is only light. Everything is washed. We breathe in the river of our light. We exhale into the heart of our light. So pure, giving, so much home, we breathe into our deepest heart. We exhale in the great well of being. All is disappearing into the all of our heart. Light is breathing in; light is breathing out. Greater and greater light, our awareness is remembering who we are. Our awareness is so much light.

The Path of Offering

*All religions have offering at their heart. More than
a meditation, it is a daily path of letting go, offering
everything in our awareness to the highest light, the
greatest love, to God. Slowly offering empties our busy
mind and brings us to the true landscape of our heart,
the little flowers, the garden of life. Meditation, more
than watching our experience, can be a cleansing of our
awareness of all that we carry, emptying us to our true
nature, discovering life's gifts that are offered to each of us.*

Meditation by another name could be called the path of offering.
Normally when we meditate, we just go into the quiet. We don't
act or react. We just be present and the great silence washes
our awareness. The path of offering is something different.
It's something very special. When we offer everything in our
awareness, it empties the mind. And as we keep offering everything
in our awareness, we come to the sacred heart, the realm of our true
nature, our light. Offering is more than a meditation. It's a practice,
moment by moment, day after day. We offer and let go whatever
we're holding on to. We offer and let go into the great silence, into
the highest light, into the greatest love. Our awareness can be quite
sticky. We easily hold on to worries and desires, expectations.
The news, our judgments, lots of things get stuck. They stick in
our awareness. The silence washes our awareness by offering us

something more. We take whatever is in our awareness, we hold it, and we offer it. It's more than a meditation. It's something we do in the middle of the night. When you wake up. We offer everything in our awareness. When we get up in the morning and during the day we remember to continually offer. Everything in our awareness we offer. The stickiness gets less and less. Our awareness becomes liquid, like a river. We want to go deep inside and offer the difficult things, the obstacles that feel stuck. They may not leave right away but just the nature of offering loosens these things. Maybe today, maybe tomorrow, maybe right now, the path of offering frees us from the busy mind. It opens the deep heart inside of us. Our personality by its nature is always grabbing on, holding, wanting. Depending upon our personality, our sticky awareness can be quite obstinate, difficult. We can hold onto things very hard, very deeply. This is why the path of offering is so liberating. We keep offering, letting go to the highest love, the highest light. Slowly our personality is not so strong.

Our practice of offering takes over. Our awareness becomes a river of light. This is our true awareness, a smooth clear river of light from deep inside of us. As we offer our everything in our awareness, we find more space inside. This big space inside allows for even a bigger offering. As we offer everything we find, we can go deeper and keep offering. We begin finding more and more light. We offer our light to the greatest light. We find more heart. We offer our heart to the heart, all, and everything. The path of offering is a calling. We offer ourselves. The little things each day, we help each other. We support each other. We keep offering our awareness till it becomes just offered. It's very beautiful. We find gifts. Each offering is a gift. Whether we're offering something difficult or something beautiful, we keep offering, letting go and offering. We find more gifts of life. When we have lost the gift of life, we have lost the path of offering. When we embrace each day as offering, each moment we offer, the gifts continue without end, big, and small.

The path of offering empties the busy mind, brings us to the landscape of our heart. Here we may find a lot of nakedness. It's okay, we offer this. The emptying of the mind brings us to a great emptiness. It's okay. We offer this emptiness. We continue to offer to the highest light. This light, our awareness, becomes more and more the same. As we continue to offer to the greatest love. We discover this love is our awareness. It's home here. It's who we are. We continue to offer everything into the great silence. No matter how noisy the world, we continue to offer and it brings us to the beauty of this moment, the simplicity of being, the gift of life itself. In our offering we discover the little flowers. They come and grow at any time and any place. It is the little flowers we offer and we grow into the garden. The garden is everywhere, inside, outside. It is in each of us. Each of us are a special part of the garden.

The Gifts of Emptiness

Free of all mental worlds, emptiness brings us to our pure awareness, the heart of who we are. The journey does not end with emptiness but begins here. The gifts of emptiness open us to more silence, peace, gentleness, humility, understanding, wisdom.... the gifts keep unfolding as we make the journey.

Meditation is a gift of emptiness. This gift is in all traditions. Pilgrims throughout all time have sought emptiness. It is emptiness that frees us from our daily story. It is emptiness that opens us to the real story, the story of our awareness, God, our soul, and all the realms of love. Emptiness is this place where there are no doors, no windows, no walls, no ceiling, no floor. Awareness just is. We're present. There's a great love here in emptiness, because all the clouds of our thoughts and busy mind have drifted away. There's a deep peace in emptiness as we go deeper and deeper into our ground of just being. Our ground of being is the ground of peace inside. Emptiness has no beginning, no ending, no border. Our awareness is one big joyous smile here.

There's no seeking, no resisting, no wanting. Simple being, everything good is present. All the mental worlds are far away. Emptiness reveals who we really are. Lots of light. the journey does not end in emptiness. Actually, the journey begins in emptiness. We spend so much time in our daily story, projecting our awareness on this and that, struggling, resisting, wanting.

Meanwhile emptiness waits for us in every moment, every day. The first step into the big journey of emptiness is to recognize the gift. Instead of wanting, seeking answers, comfort and everything outside ourselves, emptiness waits for us inside. In our culture there's not much talk about emptiness. But it is pure gold. It is the home where everything is present. It is love, safety. You can rest in infinite emptiness. Thus, the first step is to recognize emptiness, to pursue it by letting go of all pursuits, to hold it by letting go of everything else we're holding on to. We enjoy emptiness by letting go of all the substitutes for the true joy of emptiness.

The second step on the journey of emptiness is to receive the moments, one after another after another. No matter how busy the day is, how much stress, underneath it all is emptiness, present, waiting for us. Emptiness is the great silence. Every moment of silence is different. There's stillness, quiet, beauty, gentleness, openness, clarity, understanding. Wisdom. All comes out of emptiness.

How do we enter the moments of great silence? It's an attitude of humility, a breath of humility, a step of humility. We recognize that we're empty. No matter how large, important, explosive and dramatic life's adventure is outside, no matter how challenging and difficult, underneath it all it is simple, emptiness. Daily life is empty. Here is the treasure in the simplicity of the moment. We hold the simplicity of the moment in our hearts. We open. We go deeper into the heart. It is empty. We go into the emptiness. It is light. We let go and humility brings us into more light, emptiness, silence. Here we can breathe. Here our heart takes on its wings, its glory. We breathe. There is more empty space. The gift keeps unfolding as awareness unfolds forever. Emptiness unfolds forever, taking us into the many realms of love, God, so much God. It all is empty, pure, and true.

To discover the gifts of emptiness is to offer everything. This is why the pilgrims of all traditions are doing service, giving, offering. As we continue to offer all that we are, we come to who we really are. We offer everything. Here is the gold of our own awareness. This is not just gold as we know it, it vibrates with love with such a giving love. It is whole, loving, accepting, deeply loving. We offer everything and we come to the diamonds of our own awareness. It's not diamonds as we know it. It's a diamond of clarity. We can see here. It's a diamond of knowing. It's a diamond of a rich being. We offer everything and come to the gift of emptiness.

Here are all the jewels of our awareness. It's like a riverbed of jewels. The journey is one jewel after another after another. It is the jewels of life itself. This is emptiness. This is the gift of emptiness. Why would we seek anything else? What else is there? This is why in all traditions the pilgrims follow and walk the steps, offer, and surrender to emptiness. Everything is beautiful. Everything is present. No matter how difficult and challenging the daily world, the little flowers are here. The little flowers are directly connected to all the planets and the stars, the universe within us. Everyone in our lives, innocent or difficult, are little flowers. The garden has no beginning, no ending, in each of us. This awareness of life's garden is the gift of emptiness.

Building The Temple
in Our Heart

*The walls of the temple of our heart are built with silence.
As we receive the silence, the mental worlds, we carry within
us are cleared away. We come into our temple self. In the
temple of our heart there are many chapels to discover and
enjoy. There is the main altar within where everything is
given, nothing is held back. This is our sacred source.*

Meditation is uncovering our true awareness. In the unveiling,
meditation is building the temple in our hearts. The temple in our
hearts is built upon silence. The walls are silence. As we receive the
silence in our hearts, everything else is pushed away, cleared away.
The silence is the walls of the temple. No need for special prayers,
discipline, mantras or any specific religion, the silence offers us the
pure walls of our inner temple. The temple has a floor of silence.
This is simply our ground of being. The ceiling of the temple is
silence. It is totally open to all the planets and the stars. The temple
inside of us is large, very beautiful. With this ceiling being open to
all the planets and the stars, all the realms of love can be present
in our temple. Every day we want to sit in the temple of our heart
and just be. In the silence, the temple is very present, here, now. As
we go deeper into the temple of our heart, the silence is more than
peace and quiet. We discover the walls are made out of light. As

we receive the silence in all of our awareness, the light gets brighter. The silence of our heart forms a sacred temple in each of us. In the temple of our heart there are many chapels. Each of us will find our own chapels. We can walk into one chapel and it's just quiet. It can be like snow falling in the evening, pure quiet.

We want to sit in this chapel and simply be in this peace. We can walk into another chapel, and this silence is like little flowers everywhere. It's in the walls, on the ground. It's raining little flowers. We sit in this little chapel and we're being surrounded by and rained upon by little flowers of sweetness and color. They free the heart. There's another chapel in the temple of our heart, I call it the chapel of tears where we find ourselves just crying, because it's so beautiful. We cry for all the suffering in the world. We cry for all the joy in the world. We cry for all the love that is present. We cry for those who cannot cry. The tears just keep coming and coming and we realize the tears are the blood of the soul, the blood of the soul in each of us, in everyone. In this chapel we just find ourselves crying. We may not even know why.

There's another chapel that can be called the golden chapel. We walk in this chapel and we feel the golden nature of life itself. It's all in the silence. Everything, no matter how challenging or good, it's gold. This chapel reminds us of a very pure part of ourselves, our golden self. As we spend time in the silence of our hearts, the temple gets stronger, bigger, more clear in our awareness.

There's the chapel of the little children. We sit with the little children in this chapel and see innocence. We see our own innocence. We are all completely innocent, pure, clear, sweet. In the temple of our heart there are many doorways, many chapels, rooms, and the silence holds it all. As we go further within, this silence holds us, carries us, guides us to the chapel that we need right now at this moment. We sit in the sacred temple of our own heart, breathe, receive, simply be in the great silence of our temple.

As we spend time in the silence of our heart, our awareness becomes stronger, clear, brighter. Most people live separate from their heart. Awareness gets dull, stressed. Life is difficult. But as we breathe and receive the silence of our heart, our inner temple, the temple of our heart, is here, present. There are so many chapels in the heart to enjoy. We want to spend time in the main sanctuary, in the very center of the temple of our heart. We want to spend time with the altar here. In the altar in the center of the temple of our heart, everything is given. Nothing is held back. We want to spend time at the altar in the temple of our hearts. It is giving, giving, and giving more. There's no limit to the healing, well-being, peace, and love. We breathe, receive from the altar in the temple of our heart. Our awareness becomes lighter, free. The love has no beginning, no ending, There's no boundaries to our awareness.

We stay at the altar in the temple of our heart and slowly life becomes an altar. Life becomes a temple. We see it, feel it everywhere. It's incredible that deep inside each of us in the silence of our heart is a temple. And in this temple is an altar where everything is given. We share this gift together, the great silence, the sacred temple inside.

Don't Push The River

Our secret to becoming free in the river of life is to live in the heart of this moment. Instead of trying to push the river, being present in this moment in our hearts is a daily practice. Slowly we trust our river, relax, receive, feel carried in life instead of living in the stress of trying to push the river in another direction.

Today's meditation is Don't Push The River. Most people spend their entire lives pushing the river of their life. It's too much or it's not enough. It's too fast, too slow, too big, too small. We spend so much energy pushing against the river where we live, instead of just trusting, being in the river, relaxing, enjoying the river. Instead of letting the river carry us, we struggle. There's a very specific path to learn to Don't Push The River, to simply be in the river and trust. The path is a learning, a way of being very present. It's feeling this moment in the heart. It's receiving the heart of this moment. We practice being very present. Being simply in the river, not to push or pull, to stress, not trying to change it. Whether it's too much or not enough, too fast, too slow, the practice is to be right here now. This moment in our heart is a practice. Slowly, slowly we become free.

We're not pushing the river. We're not changing the river. We're enjoying the heart of this moment. Instead of talking about the future or the past, worrying about this or that. In the quiet, in the very heart of now, we come deeper into the moment of this heart. The river is all around us, inside of us. We build trust in our own heart, which is the river of our life. This is our practice, being present. As the river is warm, carrying us. We trust it. We live it. We are the river of our lives as we go further with the heart of this moment, into the heart of peace. Does it matter if there's a lot or small flow to the river? Does it really matter if it's big or small? These things become less important as we go deeper into the heart of our awareness. We are the very heart of our awareness. As we come into the heart of our awareness, the river becomes an ocean. Our awareness grows. Very, very large inside and outside, we're living in the very heart of who we are, our essence, this moment, the present. The daily story is not so big because our awareness is very big. The daily story can come and go. We can change because we are deep inside the ocean of our own awareness. The ocean of our heart which is so big. Here, inside we are held. We are safe. When we put our heart in the moment, we slowly trust the river of our Lives, easy or complicated, joyful or not.

In our heart, everything is given. This is our practice. We live in the heart of this moment, learning to receive, to enjoy, just to be. Here, now is the secret to becoming free. We don't push the river. We discover the river carrying us, holding us. The river is alive. Relax, enjoy, the river is our own awareness. There is much quietness, peace, no matter how big, fast, small, no matter what is happening in the river of Our Lives. This moment in the heart is our freedom, our home.

Bath in the Peace & Quiet of Our Heart

Meditation is not complicated. It is not something to accomplish. Meditation is a bath in the presence of our heart. Here is our beingness, heart essence, our home waiting for us to relax in, receive, and simply enjoy. Meditation bath is our opportunity for renewal, discovery, awakening, free from our daily world and personal story.

We take a meditation bath in the peace and quiet of our own heart. Actually, that's what we are always doing when we sit inside. We're taking a meditation bath in the gentleness, stillness of our own hearts. People think that meditation is complicated. There's nothing complicated about taking a bath. People think that meditation is something to accomplish. Well, we don't accomplish anything when we take a bath, we just enjoy the bath. People think that there's a special technique where we're supposed to think a certain way or relax our body or have some kind of program. A meditation bath is simply letting go, coming into the quiet of our own heart. It is all around us. It is inside of us. When we take a bath, we get naked. This means we leave our daily story, all of our busyness, all of our troubles outside. We are naked. We take a meditation bath as we come further inside, within our heart. There's more and more peace. Silence. We feel the daily world being washed away. We come into the bath of our own heart, the presence. We all could use a bath once in a while. The world is so noisy, dirty, complicated. We breathe. We come into our meditation bath, the peace, quiet of our heart inside our heart. We are coming home again. In our meditation bath we're coming to our essence. We feel the gentleness everywhere, washing away our daily worlds. The warmth of our own heart welcomes us, holds us. We can breathe again. It's beautiful to take a meditation bath, relax, and let go. As we continue to let go, surrender, we come into who we are. A big space of quiet, more space inside, we let go, relax in our meditation bath. We feel whole, complete, one.

In the quiet, there's light in our meditation bath. It is our own light, the heart inside our heart. We relax into this light. It is pure love. We soak in our meditation bath. We take our time. There's no hurry. There's no place to go. There's nothing to think about, nothing to do. We are remembering our own hearts, our own peacefulness, and quiet. The space of this peace has no beginning and no ending. Our meditation bath is full of wonder. We are free here. The peace and quiet is everywhere, inside and outside. This is meditation. This is the bath that we yearn for. The secret to a meditation bath is to be very present. The mind wanders. What are we going to do tonight? What are we going to eat for lunch, what about tomorrow, what about work. It's a habit that the mind wanders so much. In our meditation bath we want to be here. Now. We want to relax and just soak in all the quiet of our own heart. The peace, the gentleness, in our meditation bath, we just want to be present. We deserve a good bath in our meditation, in the light inside, the love here. Meditation is a gift that we want to receive every day. Let's not make meditation difficult. Life is difficult enough. Meditation is the present we give to ourselves. We come home again inside. And from here, life becomes more giving, receiving, open, caring, fun.

The Path to Nowhere

Life is full of agendas, things to do, plans, hopes, and desires. The path to nowhere is a call to be simply present. In the great now, we can let go of our busy mental worlds and find how much is here with us now, within the stillness, silence of our own heart.

Meditation is the path to nowhere. Normally we all have an agenda that we have, plans we have, a program. We are busy. We stay on the path to work, into this project, that event, the path to some place. Actually, each day is our opportunity to remember the path to nowhere, simply to be. What happens when we always have a path to someplace, some project, some event, is that when we get to the end of our lives, we don't know what to do. Our awareness is used to having a path, so focused on some outside, a climb, trail, route to somewhere. Our awareness is so concentrated, we don't know how to really open up to the big space of just being. When we leave these bodies there's a big space of love. For many people it's challenging. There has always been a path in the daily world to someplace, to some event. We've always been busy.

Meditation is our opportunity, an invitation to take the path to nowhere, just be inside. The path to nowhere is our introduction to another life. We let go of our busyness, our worrying, mental chasing of this or that. We are right here. We want to be more present than present. more quiet than quiet. To be on the path to nowhere is to truly be. Here our heart can begin to breathe. In the silence we can breathe. Our awareness is happy when it has nowhere to go but just to be here. As we come deeper in the great nowhere, our awareness finds more, more space inside. There's no beginning and no ending in this space. As we continue the path to nowhere, we come into the very heart of our awareness. There's more light. Gentleness. Openness. Clarity. We come home here, sooner or later everyone comes to the path of nowhere. It's a big joy to find it sooner, to find this big space in our heart. It is so giving. Stillness. Silence. It's important to take the path to nowhere, just to be present with our own heart. As we come deeper inside the mind gets less busy, our thoughts slow down.

As we receive the richness of our own heart, our awareness gets softer. more open. The path to Nowhere is to find everything and everywhere. just being present. It's very beautiful to have nowhere to go but to be with the heart that is here, now within ourselves and each other, all around. Yes, there is a great joy to have no agenda, nothing to do but receive the heart of this moment.

We Are Carried

*The more we are living in the heart of our awareness,
the more we realize we are carried. Our struggle and
worry are signs of too much mental living and not enough
receiving our true heart, our ocean of beingness.*

We're having a meditation on the experience of being carried. When we live in the ocean of our awareness, we have this experience that we are carried. On good days, difficult days, there's this experience that we're held, we're supported, we're carried. Everything is really okay, completely okay. There's only love There's only this infinite space of being. When we live in the ocean of our awareness, there's no big worry. There may be little worries. There are no big problems. There may be little problems. Life is not so complicated. Life is more simple. We're in the ocean of our awareness. And when we have really difficult days, it's a sign. The problem is really not about money or work or family or partner or our bodies. The problem really is that we're separate from the big ocean. The moment we return to this big ocean of our awareness, we see the problems differently. We see daily life differently. We are carried. Most people live in their heart at least part of the time. They feel the river of their life. And this is very beautiful. Sometimes the river's a little rough, or too small or difficult. The river is always changing. But we trust the river of our life. The more we live in our hearts, the deeper the trust is in the river of our life. When we go even deeper in our hearts, into the great awareness inside, that has no beginning no ending, there is more and more heart. In the ocean of our awareness, we feel carried. There's no death. There's no big fear, no big worry. We are actually carried. The presence of love is very much here. Our angels, our guides, friends, family, our community is felt. The nature and the ocean of our awareness, we feel this great support. We are being carried.

It's beautiful. In really naked times, when we feel vulnerable, this ocean is even more present. We are carried. So the question becomes, how do we live in the ocean of our awareness, the ocean of our heart? It is something we need to receive every day, good days, difficult days. It doesn't matter. We want to let go, breathe, and feel this big awareness. The moment we have a worry, instead of going into the worry, go back into the ocean and let go of the worry. Breathe and feel this big ocean carrying us.

The moment there's something, some obstacle or some difficulty, instead of diving into it, we want to dive back inside and feel the ocean of our own heart. It's so big inside, so much heart, so much awareness, just being. To live in the ocean of our awareness is a daily practice. Many times a day we let go and come back inside. Many times a day we offer what is happening in our daily life. We come back inside. Slowly we break the habit of thinking so much, being so busy, worrying so much. Slowly we become aware again, aware of our own awareness. The secret is to be present, to come back to the silence again and again, to the gentleness, the quiet inside. Here is the big ocean in the stillness of this moment. Every day we practice coming back to being present, coming back to being, now. And what is the now? It is beauty. We want to drink the beauty of life. We want to drink the heart of life. We want to be in the heart of life. Here is the great ocean. In truth our awareness is a big ocean of simply being. Beauty. Life. Simplicity. Peace. Heartfulness. Grace. We are carried in a beautiful grace. We want to feel this through our whole being. We are carried in a big big mountain of grace that's strong. It holds us. It lifts us. Each of us are carried. No matter how much we are struggling, how much we are worried, no matter how big we think the difficulty is, we are being carried.

We know this as we sit in the ocean of our awareness. Whenever we are in difficulty or a friend is in difficulty, what we can do for ourselves and each other is come back to the ocean, the great heart inside each of us. There's so much presence here, being, space for more and more awareness. The ocean of our awareness and we are being carried. So beautiful, we are carried in the ocean of our own hearts. We breathe. And we receive the great heart inside our heart. As we live in the ocean of our awareness we feel carried. In the heart of our heart, our awareness opens to more experience that life carries us. Our struggles are our resistance to being carried. Our worries, our difficulties are a resistance of the big heart inside our heart. We practice letting go. We practice receiving this beautiful heart inside our heart. We practice offering everything, just to be present now, in the quiet, the perfection of this moment.

When we live in the heart of this moment, we discover the ocean and we discover that we are carried. It's beautiful. Life carries us. And when we leave these bodies, we are carried into heaven. This is the experience. But we don't need to wait to leave these bodies. We can experience being carried here, now. It's in the very heart of our awareness. We practice being present. So much heart is here. Everyone and everything are part of the ocean. There's no competition. There's no judgment. We are all doing the best we can, letting go, resisting less, being in the heart of this moment. Here we are carried. So much grace, love, beauty. It's beautiful that we can share this together. It's beautiful that we discover the heart of this moment and the ocean where we are carried.

Bath in the Light of
Our Awareness

*Meditation is much more than watching our thoughts,
our breath, our present experience. Meditation is
a bath in the heart within our heart. Here there is
much light, brilliant, giving, pure, God within us.*

Every meditation is a return to the very heart of our awareness. We take a bath in the beauty and purity inside. Even if our awareness is full of thoughts or business, there is still light here. We want to receive this light. Meditation is much more than watching our thoughts. It's much more than following our breath, our experience. Meditation is our opportunity to take a meditation bath, and go deep inside into our heart and receive the pure light of our awareness. We may experience this light as gentleness, peace, easiness, coming home. We may need to experience the light for what it is—it's light. As we come more into our heart, we let go of all of our busyness. We offer our daily story. We offer all of our thoughts. We make the journey into this big space within our heart. It has no beginning and no ending. We breathe, and this big space of our heart, we find light. We breathe this light, the light of our awareness. as we go further within, into our heart. We hold the treasure of our own heart. The light gets brighter and brighter. We really can't even look into it. It's so strong, so brilliant. We take a meditation bath in the sweetness of our own heart. We soak in the light and the little flowers of the Garden within. We relax. We let go. The light of our heart washes us. Our thoughts spread and go away like clouds in the sky. We continue to come deeper inside. We take a meditation bath in the beautiful light of our own awareness. Holy, sacred, it completely holds us inside and outside. We can let go and fall into the arms of our own light. We simply enjoy a meditation bath. We relax, rest inside, and come home. The light of our heart is giving. It keeps giving and giving and giving. We are present, here. We receive as much as we can. It's so good to let go and just bathe in the beauty of Our Own Heart. This light is food for our nerves, for our body. It is food for our entire life. We bathe in the light of our heart. We drink this light. It is everywhere. This light is our ground of being, our source of joy. This light is the smile inside of us. The smile that never goes away. We are free here. Our meditation is a bath in the light of our own awareness.

So much heart, so much endless awareness, our meditation unveils our true heart. We keep offering everything, letting go and offering. In our heart the light gets bigger and bigger. We keep letting go, offering, and our awareness spreads and spreads into more light. Every day we can take a meditation bath in the light of our awareness, the light in the heart inside our heart. This light is special, very bright. It is our diamond mind, our wisdom. In this light are the jewels and gold, the pure love of who we are, our essence. This light is God inside of us. It is Christ. So much light, we take a meditation bath and remember who we are. All of our busy mental worlds are washed away. The light is so strong, powerful. It is true. We remember the truth inside of us. This is our journey, a meditation bath in the heart inside our heart. We simply are as much light as we are.

The Light Body

Every day the world pulls on our awareness.
Our physical body, our mental body occupy our awareness.
Meditation is our opportunity to discover and receive
our light body. Someday when we leave our physical
and mental bodies, our light body awaits us. We can
enjoy this light now, in the silence of our heart.

Let's focus, meditate on the light body within us. Every day the world pulls on our physical body. We're involved with the physical world. It pulls on our attention, pulls on our awareness. We spend a lot of energy on just our awareness occupied with the physical body, our everyday world full of thoughts. All kinds of feelings, judgments, expectations pull on our awareness. Our mental body is so busy, so full, occupying so much of who we are. Our physical body, our mental body, they occupy us. We find little chance or time for our light body. It's important that we meditate, make retreats, find time for our light body. Everyone has their own experience of the light body. It is called different names, our buddha nature, our rainbow body. It's our awareness free of this physicalness. It's free of all thoughts and feelings. It's awareness itself. The question is how do we find our light body. We breathe and go into the silence of our own hearts. The silence washes our awareness, all the thoughts and feelings, washes our identity. Our awareness spreads inside and grows. As our awareness spreads the light of our heart comes forward naturally. Usually, we're so busy with thinking and feeling and doing there's no room for the light to come forward. This is why we meditate. This is why we make retreats. We are searching. We intend to experience our light body. We come inside. Our awareness lets go of everything. In a big space, a big emptiness inside, our heart is more present. The light body may just be simple peace, quiet, openness, gentleness. As we come further into our light body, we find this love that is completely accepting. It spreads everywhere inside. The love is so thick, powerful. We just want to lay in this love, rest in this love. As all is washed in this love.

When we die and leave our body, we leave our mental body. We go into the light body. It's an incredible realm of love. No beginning, no ending, becoming thicker and thicker love. No judgment, we simply are. We cannot help but say, "yes, oh my god, yes". It's like coming home again! All our physical identity, all our emotional and mental identity comes forward. We have a life review. We are not judged in these moments. We simply melt in the light body. We don't just melt in the love completely. We still hold this physical body. We still hold this mental body. This love has to wash it. The life review that happens when we die is a big washing. We witness. We see everything we hold on to, all the physical body, the physical world, all the mental body, so much thought, so much feeling, it is all washed in this big love.

The love is totally forgiving. It holds no judgment. It's totally giving. We don't need to wait to die to come into our light body. This is why we meditate now. This is why we make retreats. We hold the intention of our light body. We come into this big space in the heart. There are no thoughts here, just being. There's no physical world here. We just are. We come more into our heart. The light gets brighter. The love comes more forward. We can totally rest here. Our awareness lets go. We soak. We receive. We're washed in this big love body.

As the filter of our physical and mental bodies gets less, we begin to see through our hearts. We begin to hear through our hearts, experience life through our hearts. Our awareness becomes clean again. Our light body is clean, free, fresh, open, giving, whole, true. We want to breathe deeply into our hearts and lay in the great love. Awareness is treasure. What do we do with our awareness? We don't want to be too busy with our awareness. We want to simply be in the heart of life, in our light body. It is our source, our treasure. It feeds every nerve inside of us. Our awareness smiles in the light body. Life is more, more of everything. This is who we are, beautiful awareness, a light body.

We want to take the time to meditate, to remember our light body. This is who we are. We come into the silence of our heart. Our awareness lets go of everything we're carrying. Our awareness spreads into more heart. Our light body is this love that is so accepting. We lay down in the love. We let go completely and simply be. Our light body is this light, so very bright. We can't even look into it. It's so bright. Our awareness is washed, washing everything until there's only the diamonds in our awareness, shining so bright. We want to remember our light body. It is our light body that frees us from so much thinking and feeling. Our light body freezes from worrying and judging. It is our light body that frees us from our physical concerns, spending so much energy organizing our physical lives. As we remember our light body, we are free. It's everywhere, inside of us, outside of us. Someday when we leave this body, when we leave our mental body, we simply are our light body. We simply say "yes", a big "yes" that has no beginning, no ending, so much light. so much presence, peace. This is the path we make. We're remembering our light body. This is heartfulness meditation. We're uncovering our hearts from all the things that keep us so busy and distracted. Each day we spend time, we uncover it completely, and here we are, naked, open, vulnerable, gentle. We celebrate the light body. We have joy. This is light.

Printed in the United States
by Baker & Taylor Publisher Services